GROWN-UP DIVAS AND DAIQUIRIS

The good, the bad and the OMG'S!

For information contact: Jennifer Kuhns, Author/Publisher http://www.jenniferkuhns.net

ISBN: 979-8-9877485-2-7

Cover design: Jennifer Kuhns
Cover Formatting Art: Steven Kistler
Formatting: Jennifer Kuhns
Editing: Rofiah Breen

PRINTED IN THE UNITED STATES OF AMERICA

Dedication

To Dad . . .letting you know that I'm going to be okay.

Love, Stink

GROWN-UP DIVAS AND DAIQUIRIS

Consider this part three as well as the continuing evolution of the life of a self-proclaimed diva who has one extra accessory--a purple wheelchair: she who retains her status of being "the other," the less than, the different . . .but now in a "more than" boss fashion. I'll explain that last part later.

Once my mom, dad and I settled in after our move to Chico, I presumed life would be pretty much be the same as it had been for many, many years. Unless you have read the two previous volumes of my autobiography you may be confused as to why a forty-something year-old person would still be living with her parents. You have to understand that I have always been somewhat of a unicorn. Ya, that fictional character with a horn in the middle of their foreheads that only exist in fairytales and make-believe worlds. Well, here I am. My wheelchair is my horn, and my Master's Degree most people believe is my make-believe world. But understand, I in fact have one of them-there Master's Degrees, and I am in fact (not to brag) highly educated. I am not deaf, dumb or blind as, I hate to say, the vast majority of people tend to believe of the physically disabled or, as I like to call "us," the physically challenged community or differently-abled.

So why do I find the need to write a third tome to the *Diva Collection*? Why do I find it necessary to expound on my life and the people around me? Well, because my assumption about my life being "pretty much the same" is and was so totally wrong!

First of all, the people around me are, as I am, getting older. I'm really specifically talking about my parents. If I'm forty-something, that makes my parents late sixties-early seventies and not getting any younger. (Although, I have to say that my mother tends to act and be younger than her age. Good or bad thing? I don't know . . .)

Anyway, because of their, I don't want to say advanced age, but my brother would say "It is what it is," discussions about what is going to happen to me when they are gone have become and continue to be more and more a topic of conversation.

Actually, that has been an underlying issue for some time, probably since the beginning of me. When I was really little, my folks, in an effort to prepare me to live somewhat independently and away from home, used to tell me that I wasn't going to live with them forever. They told me that I would eventually grow up and go off to college with my own personal aide. It was kind of a tough-love approach to things. At that age I sure as hell wasn't having it and cried every time the subject came up.

Years later when the extent of my disability was discovered, I cried again, this time not because I didn't want to leave home and go off to college; it was because I DID want to move away from home and go off to college. The reality of life for me was not usual. Just an FYI for shits and giggles, I did move away for college, but my parents moved with me as well, bought a new house and the whole shabang. United we seemed to stand . . .mostly.

I say mostly, because that elemental dialogue about what to do with me never really happened between the three of us: not just about when they were gone, but also about what happens when Mom gets too old to physically take care of me by herself. (Dad didn't do much of the physical stuff anymore because of the I'm a girl and he's a guy thing.) My dad talked to me about it, and my mom talked to me about it, but I don't think they talked to each other about it. I say that because somewhere along the way they each thought the other didn't want anyone else in our home to help or support in my daily care.

Ya, turns out Dad came up with the idea that Mom didn't want anyone besides ourselves in our home, and Mom, all on her own, aside from Dad, believed that he didn't want anyone else in our home, either. Total lack of communication, guys. They sort of each believed the other thought bringing a stranger into the home was invasive and, early on, not necessary.

So life did pretty much go on the same as it had after our move. Dad did his thing, and mom and I did our thing together. Don't get me wrong. It's not like we didn't do things as a family. Technically, since we lived a couple blocks from my sister and her family and half-again closer than we had been to my brother and his now wife, we did way more as a family than we had since my siblings and I were kids. And we had a bigger family to do it with now . . .including eating Harry Potter jelly beans.

Funny story here: When my sister and her husband were planning on moving to a new-in-the-process-of-being-built home and needing to choose flooring, cabinets, countertops, paint and so forth, a process that takes forever, we met them in Old Town Sacramento so that we could babysit their three kids for the four or five hours the picking and choosing was going to take. Our plan was to take them through the train museum. At the time, my nephew was obsessed with all trains and everything-trains, especially THOMAS. My nieces, not so much, but they also knew shopping was going to be happening as well. After lunch, potty trips and a chance to play on actual trains, we proceeded to hit up the train gift shop. My dad's pockets now a few dollars lighter and my sister and her husband nowhere near done with their picking and choosing of colors and finishes because things customarily take longer than anticipated or planned for, we still had time to kill.

(And all for not, because they never bought or moved into that house.)

As we began our slow walk down the streets of Old Town Sacramento, mostly window shopping, the kids spotted the wide-open doors of the candy store. I'm not talking a cute little single-counter candy store. I'm talking at least a two-hundred-and-fifty by two-hundred-and-fifty square-foot store full of counter-after-counter of pre-packaged, and wine-barrel after wine-barrel chuck-full of single-wrapped (what I would have called penny candy that wasn't a penny) candy. I didn't realize a kid's eyes could get so big. Of course, Grandma couldn't say no to filling a basket full of taffy of every flavor and any other candy the kids showed an interest in.

This is where the jelly beans story comes in. While perusing the rows of packaged specialty candy, my eldest niece, who was and actually still is, as a teenager, obsessed with Harry Potter, found the box of something called Bertie Bott's Every Flavour Beans. When they say Every Flavour, they mean every flavor! No, really! Every flavor! We are talking blueberry, black pepper, booger, cherry, earthworm, dirt, grapes, earwax, popcorn, spinach, marshmallow and (not that dirt and earwax aren't bad enough) vomit . . .just to name a few.

Anyway, my brother and his then-girlfriend who we had not met yet knew where we were going to be that day and showed up just after my mom and the kids emerged from the candy store, bags in hand and giant smiles on their faces, even my mom's. I remember asking her if she was nuts buying all that candy. She smiled and said, "It's not going home with us," and chuckled.

After introductions were made, and needing a break from the sun and sidewalk traveling, we all sat (well, except for me: I just rolled on over) on the lawn in the park area while the kids pulled out their loot from the candy store and started tasting the mostly gross Harry Potter Jelly Beans.

Only moments after meeting us, my brother's girlfriend was being offered half-eaten dirt, booger and vomit flavored jelly beans. We sort of knew right then and there that "this one was a keeper" because without a single split-second pause or any hesitation at all, she ate the half-eaten (probably slobbered on) gross flavored candy. Who does that? My sister-in-law! That's who!

***

Since we had already hooked up with Far Northern Regional Center and Mom and Dad had finally addressed the elephant in the room, what happens to me when they are gone, we were able to hook up with another organization called The ARC. Among a ton of other services, ARC provides respite care for those in need, paid for by Regional Centers. Of course, there is a shit load of paper work to fill out before you can even apply for respite care. And, of course, as with any governmental agency, time is not of the essence. However, in this, mine and my mother's case, timing was an issue in kind of a positive proactive way.

After going to a dermatology appointment, my mother was diagnosed with basal cell carcinoma . . .kind of a large spot on the back side of her neck. She was told the surgery needed to happen and needed to happen ASAP or like yesterday. The catch for us was that the surgery was going to take four to five hours to complete. I say catch because as a rule when my mom had any kind of appointment I either waited in the waiting room or accompanied her into the exam room. Most appointments generally last thirty minutes or less, none of which is a biggie, but four hours was a big enough deal that my mom freaked out. There was no way in hell she was going to leave me "unattended" for that long. I mean, what if I had to go pee?!

You may be thinking, why didn't I just stay at home with my father for the day? If I haven't mentioned it yet, my dad was no longer capable of physically providing care for me on his own due to a stroke he suffered a couple of years after we made the move to Chico. So that was not a viable option for us to safely use anymore. In fact, the last time Dad was able to pick me up without the XY ceiling lift and sling that was installed in my bedroom as soon as we moved in to our new home was May 12, 2020, when Mom went in for cataract surgery that went kind of sideways and took all day long instead of the half hour to forty-five minutes it was supposed to take. (There was some sort of issue with the machine that was used for the surgery and a different one had to be brought in.) I say without using the lift because, aside from the "he's a guy and I'm a girl thing," my dad was never really trained on how to operate the lift properly and flat-ass refused to use it. I fought with him for ten minutes with no positive result, for me, anyway, and gave up.

Keeping the previous episode and my dad's new limitations in mind, we panicked . . .or at least my mom did. That panic was fully heard by my Far Northern Regional Center case-worker at the time. Something that should have taken weeks to choreograph, considering the paper-pushing and people involved, took less than a week. Within that week I had my first meet and greet with my very first ever respite care provider: Amber.

(Understand that a respite care provider is different than an In-Home Care Provider, which I have now four days a week for six hours a day. I'll come back to that later.)

I was a bit nervous about the whole thing . . .about someone else other than my mother taking care of my every need. Was this going to be awkward? Was it going to be uncomfortable, embarrassing or just plain weird? I'm talkin' butt wiping weird to put it bluntly! But, Hallelujah!!!! Amber was the best first face of respite care anyone could have expected or asked for.

When she showed up at our front door, I absolutely had no idea or preconceived notion of what a respite care provider was or looked like. I didn't know if she was going to be in some kind of uniform or street clothes. Would she be just a regular kind of person or some highly professional, medically trained individual with no personality or people skills? I did know whoever it was was going to be female because I requested a female—the whole butt wiping thing, ya know. I didn't know if she was going to come all suited-up in hazmat gear because of COVID or what. But, I have to say, if I had any expectations at all, Amber shot all of them in the foot. She was absolutely my kind of peep.

This woman had on a graphic tee-shirt, a pair of black and marron patterned leggings, the required face mask, and her hair was tied up in your typical messy mom bun. She wore black flip flops, had her head partially shaved, was a thirty-eight-year-old mother of six (biological, adopted and fostered) and sported some awesome ink as well. But what impressed me the most was her "I've known you forever" mindset and approach to this all-new situation . . .for both of us.

As we sat down to get acquainted, there was no lag in conversation or awkwardness. We just began to talk, sharing aspects of our lives with each other. And I have to tell you that that suited me just fine, because if you know me, you know that I am a nosey/snoopy/curious/inquisitive/ meddlesome bitch—take-your- pick—kind-of-person. But Amber had no problem with my prying invasiveness at all. I know this because I got it right back from her. This made it really easy to move on to the real reasons she was going to spend five hours with me the next day.

The simplest of the reasons was feeding. Mom gave her a quick overview of the things I had trouble eating: lettuce, coconut, nuts, hard-candy, tortillas and such. We sat down and shared a snack, probably coffee and some kind of sweet thing. Mom told and showed Amber how she fed me: small bites, drinking from a straw, no laughing (laughing has always been a big thing for her because I tend to choke when eating and laughing at the same time). After a few minutes, Mom and Amber switched places, and Amber began to feed me. Right off the bat, we were in trouble: all because Amber asked me if I was going to spit it back out at her like her granddaughter does. How could I not laugh?! How could we both not laugh? Of course, I said no, only a second before my mom scolded us. Amber and I apologized but looked at each other, this time laughing only with our eyes.

Aside from feeding and BS-ing and keeping me entertained, the main and more complicated reason I needed someone here the next day, other than Dad, while my mom was away from home having her procedure done to remove the skin- cancer, was for bath-rooming assistance. (BTW, Amber was not the least bit shy or intimidated about learning how to use my XY Ceiling Lift and sling to get me from my wheelchair to my bath-rooming chair, dropping my pants and ultimately wiping my ass when I was done.

The one thing I do remember her saying in the middle of lift-training was "I hope you don't mind, but I'm getting hot, and I'm taking this damn mask off!" All the things that could have bothered, frustrated or disgusted Amber that day had nothing to do with me. In fact, I asked her how she felt about the butt-wiping thing, and she said, "You have nothing on my eighteen-month-old granddaughter. She is still in diapers and poops like a full-grown man!"

After that, needless to say, Amber and I were good, unlike my first day of preschool when I wouldn't let my mom leave my sight for a month, even though I had my own personal all-day every-day. Oh, how we grow!

The following day Amber knocked on the front door, and we invited her in. Mom went out the garage door headed for her appointment, and although Dad had already met Amber the day before, he still came out of his bedroom and played twenty questions with her in total Dad fashion: ya know, the typical how old are you, where did you go to school, how long have you lived in Chico, what got you into this kind of work, blah, blah, blah . . . then he looked at me with a smirk on his face and asked how his interview skills held up. "Fine," I said, but was really ready to strangle him for doing his 'Dad Thang.'

Amber picked up on my facial annoyance and asked me if we wanted to go for a walk *because it is such a nice day.* I said sure, and we headed for the door, and Dad just shuffled off back to his room satisfied with an over-the-shoulder warning not to fall off the sidewalk. Interestingly enough, going for a walk became an almost weekly occurrence for Amber and me. Luckily, CVS and Safeway are both only a couple of blocks away from my house and a common destination for us, so common that all the employees knew us by name.

My mom actually became comfortable and trusting enough with Amber and me venturing off on our own—on-foot for Amber and on-wheels for me—that she suggested we take a sort of a "road trip." Mom obviously had been thinking about it for a while, as moms do, and presented Amber and me with a plan. Her suggestion was that we drive to a local shopping center across town, shop, wander, have coffee at

Starbucks and whatever else we could find to do while she grocery shopped and did other chores, all separate from Amber and me. Mom's plan, her ultimate plan, was to have Amber learn how to load and unload me from the van in case of an emergency. Mom proposed that every time Amber and I changed locations we would call Mom, tell her we were ready to move on, and she would drive across the parking lot and pick us up, at which time Amber would load me into the van. We would then drive .03-centimeters, again, across the parking lot where Amber would unload me from the van. Mom has always believed in learning by repetition. Amber loaded and unloaded me about six times that day. We called it twelve-ins-and-outs . . .poor Amber was exhausted, but she never complained. In fact, she joked and said it was way easier and more pleasant than changing the baby-butts she had at home that she'd have to do later that day.

After that first emergency day we were able to set up with Far Northern Regional Center two hours a week respite care with Amber so that my mom could go to her appointments, or whatever, by herself and I didn't have to go and wait for her in the waiting room. I also didn't have to go to Costco and trek up and down every isle trying to dodge rude obnoxious people who acted like I wasn't even there, which is kind of a trend.

Amber was with me for about a year before her kids, jobs . . .life . . . just got too busy and unpredictable, as life does, for her to continue to do respite care. I still see her from time to time, and we pick up right where we left off, always catching up with what is going on in each other's lives.   A great friendship was forged, so unlike what was to follow with the respite care providers that came after her.

***

What came after my first 'rock star' respite home care provider and positive experience was a litany of THE GOOD, THE BAD and THE UGLY! OMG!!!!! Excuse my language, but the next few months was a total Cluster-Fuck!

After Amber had to leave, we used the same ARC extensive list of providers to find someone new. We ran into every reason, excuse, problem or whatever in the book for a big chunk of them not to be available. I get it: people have lives, things change, but remove yourself from the list of available care providers, please, and save us both some time and annoyance.

If that wasn't frustrating enough, there were the respite care providers who said that they wanted to take the job, who we set up a meet-and-greet appointment with, who either: never showed up and never called, never showed up but did call, called and said they had Covid and couldn't do it, or any variation thereof. Let us not forget the impersonal mode of communication: the blow-off text . . .not to mention the two or three people who actually did show up for the meet-and-greet but never graced us with their presence the first day of work, nor did we ever hear from them again. All of these no-shows lasted several months, and I was forced back into the Costco shopping and dentist waiting-room merry-go-round.

When we finally found our post-Amber-respite-care-provider, my mom and I were overjoyed . . .mistakenly overjoyed, we were to find out very soon. Her name was Ann.

Since we were sort of getting weirded out by the number of unknown, random people coming and going in and out of our home (or not), or at least people being given our home address, my mom and I opted to meet Ann at a local Starbucks. (If you have read my previous tomes, you know that Starbucks is better known as "the office.") This of course gave me the excuse to indulge in a latte and brownie, which became a great time filler for me because Ann was forty-five minutes late. Should that have not been a red flag!?!? Truth be known, the flag was pinkish, but, ya know, benefit-of-the-doubt and stuff-happens is probably mine and my mom's biggest downfall. We give too many chances. That might be because I often need more than one chance to do . . .whatever, myself, and maybe because I have a misplaced faith in human nature. Besides that, growing up, and to this day, if we are not fifteen minutes early to an appointment, we consider ourselves already late.

Where was I? She finally showed up with some bullshit excuse about getting her kid to school because said-kid missed the bus, backing her tardiness up with how the traffic was so-terrible. Understand, this was after multiple texts stating she was going to be five minutes late . . .each of the half-dozen times she texted. That's why I called "Bullshit." In my mind, crazy as it might be, if you are texting me every five minutes about being late, you are not even in the car on your way yet. Tell me I'm wrong.

All that aside, Ann seemed to be an okay fit. She was no Amber, but she had all the pertinent training, education and knowledge to deal and work with disabled clients. After discussing her qualifications and explaining what was expected of her, what I needed, we sat and did the friendly chat-thing for a while. Barring her first impression of being late, Ann seemed competent- and compatible-enough for the job, so we set up a second meeting to take place at our home so she could see firsthand my home environment and learn what was going to be expected of her: the lift, feeding and, let's not forget, butt-wiping to name a few of the things she would be tasked-with.

Ann was here for two hours, most of which was spent shooting the breeze and small talk with my dad-once-again-putting his famous-interview-skills to-use and learning more than we needed or want to know about Ann. She was here for so long, for no real apparent reason, that my mom and I gave each other the "when is she going to leave" eyeroll.

After the fact, the next week when she showed up for her once-a-week two-hour shift she asked me if I would sign-off on the three-hours-of-time she had spent at "the office" and here at my home. I would have called that all part of the interview process. I might be wrong, but last time I checked, no one gets paid for going to and having a job interview. Not really knowing the protocol for ARC's payroll rules and regulations, I reluctantly and stupidly signed the time sheet for her. Yup, red flag number two! I got suckered into her scam of getting paid for time she was not legitimately allowed and later realized why she had spent so much time at my home on that second day of the meet-and-greet telling us stories like how she, this grown ass woman, would pretend to speak Chinese to fool people (I don't remember the reason why) and gave us an example of her made-up gobble-de-goop language. She was trying to soak up time and money not due to her.

The next week, with colder weather coming, my main task for Ann was to put my electric blanket back on my bed and get it all plugged in and hooked up. I know, I know, I can just hear you, as a physically disabled person unable to remove an electrical apparatus from myself, such as a blanket, because of unforeseen malfunction, I should not be using an electric blanket. As my sister has said, "That is just dangerous!" On the other hand, I do have a working voice which I can and do use when I am in need of assistance, loudly, I might add. If I get too hot or too cold or have to pee or, God forbid, if I get sick in the middle of the night, my mom hears me like she has never been asleep. I don't know how she does that. It must be a mom-thing.

Anyway, during the process of plugging in the blanket, a bookshelf had to be moved. Behind the bookshelf Ann found a box of twelve heart pendants laying on the floor. I knew it was there. It had fallen a few weeks previous but at the time my mom didn't feel like moving furniture and getting down on her hands and knees to retrieve the box. Again, I knew it was there but also knew it wasn't going anywhere and I would get it out at some point in time, so I wasn't really worried about it. Ann picked up the box and opened it almost gushing over what she said were gorgeous pendants. Red flag number three is about to happen!

I talked earlier about rules and regulations for ARC respite and any other home-health care providers through any and all other agencies. I didn't know them at the time of this next incident, but I do now since I have, after the fact, seen a training manual. What I am saying is, Ann knew the rules, one of the biggies was and is "no gifts may be accepted from clients by home-health care providers."

Yes, I did! Naïve, stupid, dumb, kind-hearted, oblivious-to -life . . .I don't know what, I offered her one of the heart pendants. Keep in mind, Ann never accepted or declined the one I offered to her, but before I could even take a breath, she was on her cell phone (being on her phone is another rule broken) with not one, but both of her daughters saying that I had offered 'her' a pendant—<u>which one did they want?</u>

She basically took their orders, removed the chosen ones from the box and pocketed them. I was so fucking stunned I couldn't say a word. Then she had the gall to ask me if she could have the gold chain as well that was also in the box to which I adamantly stated "No!," which she was sort of put off by, if you can imagine that. I just let her walk off with the pendants because I didn't know what else to do. Later that afternoon when my mother came home, I ran through the scenario of what went down with Ann and the heart pendants. Mom was as shocked as I was, but as we do, giving Ann the benefit of the doubt, she questioned me about what was said and if I had somehow offered the hearts to her daughters. "Absolutely not, did not happen," was my answer. Nether one of us, at that time, knew what to do with the issue but filed it in the "keep track of this stuff file."

I don't have any earthly idea what possessed my mom and me to proceed with the next step in Ann's training the following week: the road-trip-exercise, the one where we went to a local shopping center to learn and practice loading and unloading me in-and-out of the van. There was no way in hell it would work in the same way it had worked with Amber.

I mean we really weren't a hundred percent trusting of her. But Ann seemed to be up for the training-outing, although she was pretty shaky about the whole activity. She never got to the point where she could load and unload me by herself. Because of that, my mom was forced to stay in the first store we stopped and shopped at, which meant that our plan never came to full-fruition. Instead, Mom split off from us and wandered away by herself, popping up at the end of the isle Ann and I were in every-so-often to check on us.

This was far from my experience with Amber. Amber and I were all over whichever store we were in and running through the checkout stand all by ourselves like we had been doing it for years without any trouble. Shoot, we were able to share one cart, keep our stuff separate, and without a second thought, Amber would pull my wallet out of my backpack and pay for my items as a second step after paying for her own. Not too confusing . . .one would think.

That whole inability to get me and my wheelchair in-and-out of the van was interestingly odd in itself, but that was not the red flag number 'four' moment. While perusing the section where the frames were located (I am a picture-on-the-walls-freak and have a thing for frames,) Ann picked up a package of four tea lights. Right then I noticed that she didn't have a purse, wallet, fanny-pack, anything that I thought might hold money.

Side note: At this time in my life, I did not have a cell phone. Collectively, my mom, my dad and I thought it was unnecessary for me to have a phone that I could not use by myself anyway, and whomever I was with had one. After the fact, I now know that cell phones can carry cash in a little pocket, or, even easier, you can pay for shit with an app!

Anyway, me being me, I offered to loan—emphasis on "loan"—Ann the $1.25 to pay for her tea lights. I mean it was $1.25, right?! She told me that she had money outside in the car and would pay me back once we got loaded-up. I wasn't too concerned about the money as we went through the checkout stand. Ann did fumble with finding my wallet because she didn't know where it was. (We had never even been for a walk on our own before.) The cashier put everything in one bag, and Ann and I headed-out to meet-up with my mom at the door.

Once they, together, got me loaded into the van, we toddled across the parking lot to Starbucks. I had my usual latte and brownie; mom had her regular coffee, and Ann had water. To our total disbelief, Ann said, "I just need water. I can't have any caffeine right now. I'm so overwhelmed by this experience!"

Mom and I looked at each other with a WTF expression on our faces. "For God's sake, you guys walked up and down store isles and ran through the checkout line," my mom blurted out.

Ann came back with something like, "Well, you have been doing it for forty-something years, and it's all new to me . . .and it isn't easy."

It was at that point that I mentally sighed and came to the conclusion that Ann probably wasn't going to last. I just didn't know how fast I was going to be proven right.

On our way home, as we usually do, we stopped to pick up the mail. It was at this time that I, for the umpteenth time, reminded Ann that her tea lights were in my bag, also thinking that the reminding of the tea lights would also remind her that she owed me $1.25. She blew me off again for the umpteenth time. When we got home, she grabbed her tea lights and left for the day, never acknowledging that she owed me money . . . actually, little did we know, never to be seen again.

Ann was barely out the door before I word-vomited everything that had gone down that day with her to my mom, since Mom had not been in ear-shot of Ann and me the whole time. After hearing me out, my mom was not happy on more than one level and, as mama bears do, devised a plan. I can't believe how cunning and sneaky a pissed-off mom can be. I would have never thought to do what my mom did . . .well I can, but I'm usually on the receiving end when I do something wrong. It was pretty educational and fun to see how the mind of a mad-mother works.

To begin with, my mom asked me for the receipt. She counted ten items listed. Then she counted the number of frames I had purchased which was nine. (She already knew all of this information, but she was playing the game.) She then proceeded to take a picture of the receipt and text it to Ann, asking her why there were ten items listed if I only came home with nine frames. Without accusing Ann, Mom asked if we had lost one or something between the store and home, all of us knowing full-well that the words TEA LIGHTS were listed on the damn receipt. Mom received a text back from Ann, attempting to back-pedal out of the situation, saying, "Well, maybe they scanned a frame twice or something."

Now, if I know anything about my mom, it is that you don't lie to her! I remember as a kid her telling my siblings and me, "If you tell me the truth you may get into some trouble, but if you lie to me there will be hell to pay, and you may not live to see tomorrow." At almost forty-five years old, because of that tape playing in my head, I still weigh the pros-and-cons of what-to and not-to share with my mom . . . and have a tendency to over-share.

Ann poked the bear with that one little sentence and broke my mom's first and foremost cardinal rule. Within the next two text messages Ann was called out, not necessarily for lying but for being less than honest. In the first text back to Ann, Mom asked, "What is this tea lights thing on the receipt?" OMG, all I could do was giggle and wait. Ann had no understanding that she had been given either a chance to come-clean or enough rope to hang-herself. She seemed to have chosen a combination of both. There was a brief pause, what I'd call a guilty pause, before Ann responded, "Oh, yeah, I got those and forgot to pay Jenni back. I'll get that to her next week when I come." The funny thing is, next week never came.

Needless to say, my mom's feathers were pretty ruffled by the text conversation. That, added to the pendant situation, sat kind of sideways for her. As a parent of anyone disabled, there is always a fear for that or those parents or even other family members of people taking advantage of a person in need of respite or home health care. After mulling it over in her mind for a few days, Mom discussed with me the options we had concerning Ann. Basically, we decided to let her go. There was no trust.

As it turned out, we didn't have to employ any of our options. Ann texted the day before her next shift with a long boo-hoo story about how her family needed her right now and that for her to work outside of the home was just too stressful and was causing a great amount of hardship for her them. Personally, I think she was embarrassed that she got caught in a lie and for basically stealing the whopping $1.25 from me which she didn't mention about paying back.

My mom replied with a short one-line text: That is fine. It saves us from letting you go. The next string of text between Ann and my mom bounced between indignation from Ann to matter-of-factness from my mom. Ann, of course, wanted to know why we going to fire her. My mom laid it all out to her: the pendants she took for her daughters that were not offered to her daughters, the $1.25 and every other weird thing Ann had done that my mom could think of. Lots of other words were said, ending with Ann stating that she would return the pendants and bring back the money.

A couple of days later, I happen to see her drive up outside my bedroom window and park on the street without turning her car off. She walked up to the front door with a small bag in her hand, set it down and turned and walked back to her car and left. She never knocked or let us know she was there. Mom went out and got the bag and brought it in to me. She dumped the contents out onto my bed. We stared at two heart pendants and five quarters, and we both broke into a fit of laughter. All I could think was wow, all over pocket-change.

I have to add here, at this point, that as a disabled person (or not) I will admit that I tend to bond with people WAY TOO FAST . . .well, with most people who come into my world and act as extensions of myself. I basically put my life and trust in their hands for the duration of time they are with me.

They sort of become part of my family unit. Weird, I know, but when someone is literally spoon-feeding you and wiping-your-butt, a certain amount of familiarity develops and grows rather quickly. So, I guess I am owning up to the fact here, the truth, that all things that happen between any given care provider and myself is not always all the care provider's fault. I over-do everything. I over-share. I over-give. Hell, I suppose I even over-love.

***

As I sit here thinking and writing about this, I can't help but look back at another thing that happened with Ann, a thing I did, a thing she was strangely okay with and shouldn't have been, (WTF was I thinking?) .

. . a thing before the pendent and candle things. What was it? Well, after knowing her for like three weeks and working on designing my Christmas cards one day and getting them ordered, I asked her to pose with me for a picture to be added to the card. So dumb! Why did I do that?! She wasn't family or a friend. She was more of an acquaintance at that time. But that is me and my . . .what should I call it . . .some kind of attachment-disorder. The truth be known, she was gone before the cards were even delivered. The ah ha moment, not in a good way, was when my mom opened the package and saw the pictures on the cards. All she said was "REALLY?" I felt pretty dumb. Needless to say, lesson learned. This year's card has a picture of me and my dog.

***

Once again Mom and I were on our own. It was several weeks and many, many phone calls later. By this time a good number of providers had dropped off the respite care list or had full time positions and couldn't take on any new clients. Finally, we hooked up with a woman named Joie.

The initial phone call was pleasant enough. We chatted on speaker-phone, and I shared what I needed, and Joie shared a little about herself. She told us she had other clients she worked with and that she dog-sat and, among other things, wanted to open a boarding-kennel in her home. My first phone impression of Joie was that she was an upbeat, animal-loving, slightly older funny kind of a woman. When she showed up for her first training shift my impression was slightly altered. She was, in fact, upbeat, funny and an animal-lover, but she was one of the tiniest, little women I had ever met . . .and she was older than my mom with a bad back, bad knees and bad heart. The only

44

reason I know about her heart was because when my dad met her for the first time, they discovered that they had one of the same cardiologists. That was a bit spooky. I had visions of Joie having me hanging up in the sling, literally hanging, and her having a heart attack and ending up on my bedroom floor passed out leaving me yelling for help . . .for the help. Luckily, that never happened.

Joie was only with me for a couple of months (I'll explain why only a couple of months in a minute), and my vision never came to fruition, but the problem was that Mom could never leave. Mom could go outside in the backyard and work in her pottery shed where she had a baby monitor so that I could call her if I needed help. She could of course listen in on conversations if she wanted to, as well, although she never really did. She was usually too absorbed in pot-making, getting ready for whatever next holiday was coming up. She was very tuned into hearing her name being called: Mom,

Mitzi, Grandma or whatever, though, and was quick to respond.

The problem was that Joie could never figure out how to properly use the -sling and lift. Well, the lift she got. It was the sling that she had a major issue with. Let me explain . . .

In the first two volumes of my autobiography, I mentioned the XY ceiling lift and sling that I use to get to-and-from my bed and to-and-from my bath-rooming/bathing chair. The first MUST when using the sling is that the upper portion of the sling and straps have to be placed under my arms. The second MUST is that the bottom straps have to go around my legs so that I am in sort of a sitting position. That way all four of my limbs are securely-supported, and I can be safely lifted from my wheelchair, have the appropriate-clothing removed (pants down to pee), and have my body lowered into the bath-rooming chair.

Sounds easy, right? Bless her heart! Not so much for Joie. She never understood the placement of the underarm straps. She always wanted to place the upper straps over or around my arm, wrapping me up like a burrito.

Just to share, I have always had a safe word: CAKE. Weird safe word, I know, but my dad told me a really long time ago that I should have a word that is short, sweet, easy for me to say that has shock-value. I mean, why would I yell CAKE while going to the bathroom?! Whoever is doing whatever is going to stop when they hear me yell CAKE.

Anyway, the first and only time I ever used my safe word with a care-provider was with Joie. One day, near the end of March of 2022, I didn't catch her in time. She once again had the upper portion of my sling wrapped around my arms. We were chatting, as we usually did, and she lifted the lift and moved me over towards my bath-rooming chair. Before she even started to lower me down into the bath-rooming chair my entire body started to ooze down and out of my burrito-wrap. I screamed—CAKE—a little too late. My back hit the chair, hard, and my head was where my butt should have been with my legs still up in the sling two feet or so above the rest of my body. What I heard next was Joie screaming, "MOM, MOM, MOM!" to my mom. Joie was absolutely frantic, and I remember telling her, "I can hear my mom coming; she is on her way, but you need to calm down." That's what I was telling Joie while I was totally freaking out on the inside for a couple of reasons: all my parts hurt, and I peed my pants!

When my mom got to my bedroom, she stood with a WTF look on her face for a split second. It only took her a second more to figure out how to get me out of the situation I was in. She lowered the sling down to where my legs were even with the rest of my body and then hoisted my upper body into a sitting position. (Her years of power lifting always comes in handy.) Thinking I still needed to go to the bathroom, my mom rearranged "things" and lifted me back up to drop my pants. "Mom, never mind, I already peed," I said.

"Alrighty," she answered. "We'll get that taken care of."

"Am I fired," Joie asked. Mom didn't answer and told us that she was going to go out and finish what she was doing and come back.

When my mom came back into the house, Joie proceeded to tell her, "That's it. I'm firing myself. That was too scary, too dangerous, and I'm done."

And she was.

I was really sore for a couple of days, and every time I coughed, sneezed or laughed I looked like I was dying. I thought I broken a rib and wore a wrap for a day or so until I could get into see my doctor. Turns out the wrap was exactly the wrong thing to do since I had a deep muscle-bruise and not a broken rib. The doctor said that I needed to be able to fully-expand my lungs or "whatever" to fully-heal. It took a good six weeks for me to be able to breathe without thinking about it.

Joie called every few days to see how I was doing and apologized profusely every time. Two years down the road and we are still great friends, see each other every so often and keep in touch through Facebook. We even joke about how she dropped me.

***

The day after Joie fired herself, I had an already-scheduled home-visit and review/evaluation with a woman named Ximena, my case worker at the time, from Far North Regional Center here in Butte County. Every county has a Regional Center to contact for help and support. You might have to ask questions over and over and maybe even fight with them a little bit, but it is a great place to start to get the information support needed.

Here is an example of what I'm talking about. Over the years, my parents and I had asked my case workers (a new one most every year, which explains the lack of continuity in that workforce and the lack of build-up of acquired knowledge by them) the same questions about home-care for me while my parents are still here, versus when they are no longer on this earth. Our answers were always non-answers. The case workers always seemed to fumble around the question and end up saying, "Well, I don't know. I'll have to ask," and then never get back to us. So annoying . . .

That is until Ximena, my newest case-worker showed up. We asked the same "what if" questions, and low and behold . . .she had the answer right there on the tip of her tongue ready to spit it out at us. "I don't know why no one else shared this information with you. We all have access to it." Then she added, "I've had to look into this because I have other clients who require similar outside-of-family support."

Within the week I received an email from Ximena with a list of something called SLS—Supported Living Services. It was a definite OMG moment for us! I now know that every county should have and provide these services. Ya just gotta ask the right questions of the right people, which means you have to ask everyone all the time until you find that right person with the answer you need.

In Butte County, where I live, this is the list of SLS providers and support programs that are available, not just to the disabled community but to the community as a whole (I guess I'm talking about old folks here who need supported help in living, although this might be an assumption, and we all know what happens when you assume):

Butte County SLS Providers

Mains'1

COMPASS

PosAbilities

AMJaMB

California Vocations

Personal Assistance

Here's The Deal

Partners In Care

Day Programs

-Adult Day Programs and Community Integration Program

-Work Training Center

-ARC of Butte County

-Mains'1 Innovations

-Mains'1 7th Street Center for the Arts

We spent a couple of days going over the list and perusing the different websites comparing my needs to what each "company" provided in the way of services. My mom and I ended up going with Partners In Care because what they provided seemed to mesh best with the level of care/assistance that I require. After making our choice known to Ximena, the very next day a woman named Susan called and made an appointment with us for the following day to go over . . .all the things. This was on a

Thursday morning. On the following Monday morning, April 3rd, 2023, just four days later, Susan arrived with my first Partners In Care personal-assistant, Sharon, at ten a.m. How easy was that, having the right person to ask the question that needs to be answered show up on your doorstep and get you what you need in only a week's time? And I have to tell you, this couldn't have happened at a better, most timely point in our—my mother's, father's and my—life.

***

As you may recall, I mentioned earlier that my father was having some health and mobility issues of his own, and my mother was spending most of her days bouncing back and forth tending to me and my needs and my father and his needs. I can't help but think that her life was pretty sucky during that time. So, having the addition of a personal-assistant/care-provider in the home to take care of and support my needs was absolutely monumental! Or so I thought . . .and it was . . .at the beginning.

The beginning being the first four months from April 3rd, 2023 to August 2nd, 2023 while my dad was still at home, prior to being taken to the emergency room by ambulance, for the second time, and then admitted to the hospital, where he was finally diagnosed with stage-four blood, bone and brain cancer.

Needless to say, that was a WTF moment and explained all of his physical and mental "weirdness" that had been going on for some years. Eventually he was transferred to an assisted-living facility with hospice support super-close to home.

That is when things with Sharon went off the rails.

So, here is my hindsight view . . .Sharon had enough brains to keep herself semi-professional for the first four months of her employment in our home. She did have some off-the-wall, less-than-ideal, odd, whatever you want to call them, instances, beliefs, ideas about, let's just say, numerous things.

The first example would be when my mom lent her a bunch of cooling towels that you freeze and then wear around your neck (or wherever) along with a few other things. She was going to an outdoor concert sometime in the hot month of June.

Now, I was raised that if you borrow something you always return that item in as good or better condition than you borrowed it. When Sharon returned to work on the following Monday she did bring and return the borrowed items. The problem was, and this is gross, after wearing them in 100-plus-degree heat and sweating all over them for several hours, SHE DID NOT WASH THEM BEFORE SHE RETURNED THEM. She said that she got home late and didn't have time to wash them. Who does that? I mean, wash them, and bring them back on Wednesday. (She didn't work on Tuesdays for personal reasons, and I had someone else on Tuesdays. I'll get to that later.) Obviously, my mom and I were more than a little taken aback by her flippant actions and attitude about the whole thing. Strangely enough, or not, that wasn't the only thing she borrowed and returned dirty. Yup, red flag number one.

The first totally off the wall thing Sharon said to us was, "I'm gonna be part of your family pretty soon."

I remember my mom and I looking at each other and my mom saying, "Nope, we may become good friends but not family."

Sharon responded, "Oh, yes, I will. You'll see."

When Sharon turned to look at me, my mom mouthed, "No fucking way!"

It wasn't too long before Sharon started calling herself 'Kid Four.' (My mom has three kids.) Attachment issues much? Red flag number two.

Not only did Sharon think that she was going to be part of my family, from my point of view she thought that she was my mother and had no problem interrupting a conversation going on between my mother, father and Susan. The meeting wasn't even about me. My mom and dad were having a meeting regarding setting up care, also through Partners In Care, for my dad because of his declining condition. Sharon had the gall to abruptly call out my postural, shall I call them, short coming. "Jenni, hands down and head up," even when my mother was sitting right there! No doubt she had heard my mom say those things to me in the privacy of our home, since she was here six hours a day, but never in public or in front of people. Not only was it embarrassing, it was not her place to do so. If fact, my mother would have <u>never</u> called me out in front of people in that way. My mother, bless her heart, has always been very discreet about prompting me about . . .things, in public or in front of people. When I let my head flop to the side, she looks at me and acts like she is cracking her neck, and I know exactly what that means. But I am the only one who sees it and knows what it means. When I talk, I most often throw my hands up somewhere around my ears and sort of, no, not sort of, I plain-ass stiffen. If I didn't have a seatbelt on, I would probably stand up and throw myself out of my wheelchair. My mother, again very discreetly, kind of does a little butterfly hand flutter that no one else but I see. (If you are old enough to remember the movie *8 Seconds* with Luke Perry playing the part of

Lane Frost, you'll understand how I equate my mom's hand movement with that of Lane's to his wife who is the only one who understood his hand jiggle.)

Mom and I both were dumbfounded by Sharon's show of, I guess I'd call it, authority over me . . .like I was a child who needed to be corrected for bad behavior. At the time we let it go because we were, first of all, shocked and were all sitting in front of her boss and didn't want to cause her any embarrassment or criticism. Hind-sight—we should have. After Susan left, my mom did confront Sharon about her outburst and the unacceptability of it. Red flag number three.

The next semi-show of perceived authority Sharon thought she had was during my 'standing-sling' time. Because I spend every-day all-day sitting in a wheelchair, my hip-ball and socket get a little sloppy or loose or however you want to phrase it. Therefore, several times a week, I get hitched-up to a sling that allows me to stand. While in the sling, I am able to put pressure on my feet and legs and stand, which helps the hip-ball stay better placed in the socket.

Now, after working with therapists and, because of my mom's acute knowledge of ME, we had the strap-loops set at the precise settings which provided the best posture and support for my needs. One day out of the blue, Sharon decided and announced, "Let's try this other loop." Luckily, because we have baby-monitors (a poor man's intercom system) all over the house and in Mom's pottery shed, she heard the comment and came running into the house and into my bedroom. "What the hell are you doing?!" was her greeting.

"Well, I just thought we'd try a different loop," was Sharon's unabashed answer.

"Listen," my mom, not so calmly replied, "the loops that we use we use for a reason. They were not arbitrarily chosen. They were chosen because it is the best fit for Jen. You have no reason to fuck with what you don't have knowledge about. When you show me your Physical Therapist license then maybe we'll talk."

"Well, I just thought . . ."

"Well, don't . . ." and Mom walked out.

This was one of those 'you don't want to mess with a mama bear' situations. Needless to say, I never said a word. I knew better . . .

Another bothersome issue I had with Sharon was her smoking. She never smoked in our house, which was a good thing, but early on she did ask my dad if she could go outside and smoke after lunch because she was allotted a fifteen-minute break at some point in the day. He said it didn't bother him and he didn't care. So she took that and ran with it as a yes. Now, in my thinking, she was working for and with me and not my dad. I'm the one who had to smell the smoke residue when she was done with her smoke-break.

The problem with that situation is something that I'm pretty sure, I'm going to say, most disabled people—who live at home with parents or other family members who own the house, pay for groceries, pay household bills, etc. (and who might even have in-home care providers)—feel that they have no say or authority in what happens in their space or in the home they live-in. I, for one, even at forty-three years old, was not going-against what my father, my parent, told Sharon. I felt that I not only had to live with it but that I also had to live with Sharon smoking once a day after lunch and then unilaterally increasing her smoking time to every twenty to thirty minutes throughout the day. Can I call red flag number four here?

***

 I hate to come off as being knit-picky, but let's talk about food. Again, I, as a disabled person, a person who must depend on others for my very existence, really have no control over . . .pretty much anything. I do remember as a kid bringing home the school hot lunch menu for the month and deciding "for myself" what days I did and what days I didn't want a hot lunch. After saying what I just said about not having control, I have to step back a bit and say that my parents did, in fact, not just allow, but expected and encouraged me to make decisions for myself and to express my opinions, wants and desires (some of which they would regret later, like my desire to raise and show sheep . . . something I did for ten years). Those decisions might have been on a small unimportant scale back then for some, but any decision I made or make now was and is a big deal. Sorry, off topic again as I tend to do.

Anyway, let's talk about food. Now, I like pizza as much as the next person. But I don't like it EVERY DAMN DAY OF THE WEEK! Yes, she did!

The first few months Sharon was here my mom always had some sort of a meal plan in place. I've always had my favorite go-to lunches—probably not the most acceptable, healthy, lalalalala, meals on the planet . . . but, as I said, my decision. I usually had something like a yogurt spinach dip with crackers, coffee and a brownie, mac and cheese, an occasional fish fillet from McDonald's, and, of course Moon Pies. Do y'all know that Moon Pies need to be microwaved for ten seconds to make the perfect smores delight? Sharon didn't know. I had to teach her that one.

After my dad was transferred from the hospital to the assisted-living facility things were very different. You would have thought life would have become, I don't know, maybe easier or smoother, but no, it wasn't. My mom spent the six hours a day (when Sharon was here with me) with my dad at the assisted- living facility. I'm not going to go into detail or specifics on this, but I got why my mom was there. This is when pizza became an almost daily "thing."

Pizza was, and I'm sure still is, one of Sharon's favorite foods. She ate it every chance she got, which meant I had to eat it with her if I was going to eat at all. When lunch time rolled around, I wasn't asked what I wanted. I wasn't asked what was available. I was informed in a conversation that went something like this:

Sharon: I don't know what you want for lunch, but I'm

ordering pepperoni pizza to be delivered.

Me: Do we have to have pizza again? We've had it two days this week already. I don't really want pizza. I don't like it that much.

Sharon: Oh, well. Do you want to eat?

To top that off, I found out that "my" home address was Sharon's default address on the pizza ordering app, which is absolutely and totally against the rules and regulations spelled out in Partners In Care Policies and Procedures. They are adding up. Red flag number five.

Of course, these may seem like small minor bumps or annoyances compared to what happened with Ann, but we really should have paid more attention to them because mole-hills, those bumps and annoyances, can become mountains so quickly that you don't even realize when it happens. And it did happen. There were so many more instances with Sharon that I could write a whole 'nuther volume about just that. For example, the activities that I wanted to do during the day, like walking to CVS, that is two blocks away from my house, weren't happening because Sharon's foot hurt. Or, straightening out my clothing cubbies: all the pants together, and all the shirts together, and all the sweaters together, so I could see ALL of my clothes, because Sharon said, "They are fine; it doesn't matter." Well, Damn it! Do I need to say it again? There is very little that I have control over, and being able to choose my own outfit for the day can only be completed if I have total visual access. So, YES! it does fucking matter to me! And it is not fine! I don't even know what flag number this is …

I guess my point here is that I was beginning to feel like I was being . . .hmmmm . . .what? . . .ignored, or at least my wants and desires . . .controlled . . .what I could or couldn't do, eat or even think . . .and what I had to 'put up with' like the smoking. Not even beginning. I just was.

At the same time, I really didn't know what control or rights I actually had in the client/care-provider relationship. I didn't really have a clue what was normal or acceptable in this situation. Is what was happening customary? Was the care-provider the boss, or was I? I felt like I was in a catch-22 position because my mother needed to be with my father and if I made too much of a fuss about Sharon or called Sharon on her actions, I was afraid that she would quit. So I never told my mom any of my concerns or what was going on. I mean, it wasn't like my mom didn't have a huge plate full of shit to deal with with my dad basically dying of cancer. She needed to be with him. In my mind, I had to put up with "it." What choice did I have? I had no other choice.

***

Remember how I mentioned Sharon didn't work on Tuesdays? Well, that was a whole different kind of day. Very early on I called it 'My Mary Day.' On Mary-days I was in charge. I decided what we were doing, which was not sitting on our ass playing shoot the bubble or whatever stupid game other care-providers have been known to do. Always first on my Tuesday agenda was to clean up the cubby mess. The funny thing is, the jumble of clothing that Sharon created sometime during the four-days-a-week she was there drove Mary as bonkers as it drove me. Mary understood my (not that I have been diagnosed with it) OCD need for neatness, order and the ability to see my clothes.

Although the three of us, Sharon, Mary and myself, were within a few years of each other age-wise, my relationship with Mary was more of a friendship, whereas my relationship with Sharon was more often her being a controlling-mother, which only became worse as time went on.

The first Tuesday Mary arrived for work, as always when a new person is introduced into any situation, was a little awkward. Unlike she did with Sharon, Susan did not accompany Mary to our first meeting. We were on our own. There is always an ice-breaking period to get through, and it turned out that we were okay and did just fine, kind of better than just fine.

At this point in time, my dad was still at home, so my mom (this will make more sense later), once again and as always with a new person, spent the first couple of days familiarizing Mary with my routines: feeding, bath-rooming, using the XY ceiling lift which is always a biggy so I didn't get dropped **again**, activities, pet care (I have a dog) and so forth. After a couple of Tuesdays, when Mary and I were finally left to our own devices, when my mother felt secure enough to go about her business and run errands, we found that we had an immense amount in common. We spent pretty much the entire time sitting at the kitchen island, not doing anything, mind you, but talking and sharing and laughing non-stop, laughing so much that my dad made his way, unsteady as he was, out of his bedroom, and asked, "What are you girls laughing about?" Every day that Mary was here my dad always found a reason to come out and visit with us for a bit.

During one of our first share days, we talked about *Days of our Lives* and how it was our favorite soap opera and how we would both record it on a VHS tape using a TV/VCR combo and then watch it when we got home from school, the very first thing like our life depended on it. When I told her that I met Bo Brady at a Target grand-opening in my hometown, she turned green with envy. You can only imagine what she said and did when I showed her the pictures of Bo and me together, then telling her that I knew before anyone else in the whole world that PRINCESS GINA WAS IN FACT HOPE WILLIAMS BRADY.

As silly as that all might sound, what I'm getting at here is the idea that Mary wasn't trying to be my mother, my boss or my decision-maker. We were interacting, not like I was disabled and she was my able-bodied care-provider. We were becoming true and fast friends. It's almost two years later now, and my mother is very rarely surprised (much to her chagrin) at anything Mary and I come up with. She, on more than one occasion, has described Mary and me as acting like two twelve-year-old boys.

It wasn't long before I felt comfortable enough to share with Mary how and what was occurring with Sharon. All the things I had questioned in my own mind over many months I brought up, soliciting Mary's opinion about. I asked her if whatever Sharon was doing was okay, because this whole situation of having someone assisting with my care for more than two hours a week was a whole new rodeo for me. Surprisingly, I discovered that there was a laundry-list of things Sharon did, didn't do, said, didn't say, that was not kosher. Besides the things I mentioned earlier, the list goes on . . .like these:

1. Instead of walking beside me and interacting with me, she walked behind me, smoking or vaping (which was totally against PIC rules).

2. At times, she sat on the couch all day long "because she didn't feel good," doing nothing, which meant I did nothing.
3. The only fucking time my mom asked Sharon to make sure I was fed and bath-roomed (because we had a play to go to), she decided to do her own pottery-work, instead. When Mom came in and asked if I was fed and so-forth, Sharon had the audacity to say, "Oh, I forgot." I didn't get dinner until nine o'clock that night.
4. She actually asked me if I liked Mary better than her! That was minutes before she quit.
5. Sharon and I were supposed to go in together to get my mom a "you need to de-stress" gift. I gave my half of

the cash. The gift was never purchased or given, and my money was never returned.

6. During Mary and my Friends-Giving (the day after my dad died, two days before Thanksgiving), after an un-invited Sharon showed-up and drank all of our party-booze, and while my mom was going through the food that my dad had had in his room, Sharon informed my mom that she would take all of the Ensure for her husband (who also had cancer at the time). It wasn't an ask; it was an "I'm telling you." If you knew my mom, that didn't happen. I remember her saying to Mary and me that she would drink the gross stuff herself, first, before she would give it to Sharon.

There are just way too many more instances for me to mention, and the last of those brings me to my mom's list. The funny thing was, my mom had her own list of, I'll call them irritating things that Sharon did, didn't do, said, didn't say. Some of them I knew about.

The one that I best remember, the one thing I always tried to talk Sharon out of doing, was assuming that she had the authority to get on our home-computer. (She assumed a lot of shit.) She would go as far as to log my mom out of her email account, sign herself into her own, do whatever it was that she was going to do, and then sign my mom back into her account. This time the problem was that Mom had changed her password. Not only couldn't Sharon get Mom signed back into her email account, but she had tried so many times that all future attempts were blocked. (There was a twenty-four-hour waiting period before the password could be re-established.)

When my mom came home from running errands, saw what was going on, got mad, slammed a full cup of coffee on the counter and left the house, Sharon had the gall of getting upset and crying and yelling at me . . .like it was my fault. She threatened not to come to work the next day because she said she couldn't keep walking on egg-shells around my mom . . . leaving me hanging.

I won't even bring up the fact that Sharon's conducting her own personal business on my time, not to mention on my computer, is totally outside the realm of accepted rules and policies of Partners In Care. (Ha, I guess I just did.)

But some of the things on my mom's Irritating-Things list, I honestly had no clue about, really, until after my dad passed away, because my mom was no longer spending hours upon hours away from home and with my dad at the assisted-living facility. On that list there were things like Sharon walking into our house without knocking and then complaining if the door was locked so she couldn't just walk in, or her going through our mail and then divvying it out like she owned it, or her pulling a picture that was attached with Command tape off of the wall and pulling a chunk of plaster off with it . . .AND THEN TRYING TO HIDE IT like a three-year-old. (When I shared Sharon's statement with my mom about the plaster, "Not a big deal. Not my house," Mom was less than happy about it.)

Oh, and then I remember the time I decided to dye my hair (it looked good, btw) and my mom coming home and seeing the dye all over the bathroom wall.

Anyway, back to me and my list: every item I brought up, Mary definitively said, "NO!" Probably more of a "Hell, no, that's not okay!" For some weeks she listened to my complaints, commiserating with my dilemma, until I suppose she couldn't stand it anymore. One day she, I have to laugh after the fact, in a pissed-off, motherly, I love you sort of fashion, an ultimatum for your own good, if you will, told me that I needed to tell my mother what was going on with Sharon and if I didn't, she was going to because what was going on with Sharon and me was unacceptable.

When my mom came home that afternoon after spending the day with my dad, where she spent most every day, I begrudgingly laid it all out on the table with Mary's help. My mother sat quietly while I shared with her all the things I had shared with Mary. Dismayed, all she said was "Why didn't you tell me any of this before?"

"Because you were kind of busy," I answered. "And I figured that I could deal with it for awhile."

"Well, not anymore!"

From that day forward I promised Mom that I wouldn't keep any Sharon information or secrets from her. I promised to share all things, things that happened, things that were said or done, or things I didn't approve of or agree with. So, every day we would have a "Sharon debriefing" as we called them.

It was at this precise moment that I decided that it was time for me to confront Sharon, on my own, about her smoking habit. Although I missed my dad immensely and wished more than anything that he was well and here, I also had a new-found, liberating feeling of control over my surroundings . . .my living environment. I explicitly told Sharon that I didn't appreciate the amount of time that she spent smoking and that I absolutely hated the smell of smoke on her when she came back into the house. She seemed to be a bit stunned by my comment. She proceeded to try and defend herself with a statement about my dad saying it was okay for her to smoke after lunch, at which point I stared at her and said, "He isn't here, and you don't work for him, anyway, and after lunch is only one time." The next time Sharon came to work, she no longer smoked but used a vape-pen. I'm not sure that is any better, but at least I didn't smell it. She still took more smoke-breaks than allowed (as outlined in the written rules and regulations of her employee's manual), but I took that as a win. I mean my voice was just in its infancy stage, and I was able to make a change to my circumstances . . .to my liking. I felt a little proud and maybe just a little smug, all at once.

***

On November 20, 2023, at 5:30 a.m., three days before Thanksgiving and my brother's birthday, my mom got a phone call from the hospice nurse at the assisted-living facility. My dad had just passed away. Why am I mentioning this? Because this time, this event, if you will, had been discussed for several weeks prior, to ensure all of everyone's ducks were in a row. My mother and both care-providers developed a plan, specifically so that I would be taken care of without having to go to the assisted-living facility with my mom.

The plan was that Mary would be called first because she lives the closest to us. In her P.J.'s, she would be here within ten minutes and then my mom would immediately go. Then Sharon would be called, and she would be here as soon as she could (she lived 40 minutes away), since it was one of her days to work. How does that saying go—the best laid plans of mice and men—:that's how our plan shook-out.

The actual first call my mom made was to my sister who lives two blocks away from us. She had also spent hours and days with my dad over the last four months. Mom told her that Dad had passed, and my sister immediately told my mom that her husband would be right there to hang with me and that she would go to the facility, meet up with the hospice nurse and wait for Mom. My mom tried to explain that we had a plan in place and her husband didn't need to come and miss work. "He's in the car and on his way," was her way of shutting-down any more conversation or push-back from my mom . . .which was a good thing because Mom was a mess, and it turned out to be the best decision.

The first call I had my brother-in-law make was to Sharon to let her know that Dad had passed. She knew why I was calling because it was 7:30 a.m. on a Monday morning. It took me a little bit to convince my brother-in-law to call someone that early in the morning because the family has this unwritten rule that you don't call anyone before 9:00 a.m. unless it is an emergency. At that particular moment it wasn't an emergency because everything was basically handled. Anyway, after explaining that I was taken-care-of for the moment, Sharon said she would be here ASAP. I wrongly assumed that she would arrive within the hour. She showed up at 10:00 a.m., the beginning of her regular work-day. Really? That's ASAP?

What made that day even more complicated was that a new hire care-provider was coming that morning to be trained as a back-up for Sharon or Mary, when needed. Katie was her name. After Katie arrived and my brother-in-law left, I opted for a shower. This had not ever been something tasked to Sharon or even Mary in the past. The reason for the shower was because I had peed on myself. Not feeling comfortable asking my brother-in-law for help in that aspect, since he had never done it before, and being that I was told that Sharon would be here "as soon as she could," I opted to wait for Sharon to show up, which was way later than I thought was planned. Not that I'm blaming her for my accident, but be here when you say you are going to be here. I would have done something differently.

Katie's training started as soon as I was wheeled out of the shower and to the toilet. The XY lift was used and explained. How to get me from the bathing/bath-rooming chair to the electric wheelchair was explained. The feeding and drinking process was shown and explained and so forth. The few hours Katie was here was pleasant enough. I even like Katie. I did find it interesting, though, that Sharon didn't pick-up on the fact that Katie is freaking deaf . . .or at least extremely hearing-impaired. I knew the moment Katie opened her mouth that she had a hearing problem, just by the tone of her voice.

On the other hand, Sharon, she who claimed to know all about every disability known to man, never picked up on the fact that Katie was hearing-impaired. She continually snapped at Katie for doing what people with hearing issues do . . .and kudos to Sharon for wanting to include me in the conversation, but she had no clue as to what was going. I knew right away why Katie was looking at Sharon instead of me: she was reading Sharon's lips.

Moving on, here is the lead-up to the final red flag on the field. While I was in the bathroom, one room away from where the two of them were talking (visiting, I suppose), I heard Sharon tell Katie, "Ya, she is a real bitch. I have to walk on egg-shells around her." Sharon never knew that I overheard her comment, and I opted to lie to my mom by omission, breaking my promise by not telling her what I had heard.

In addition to talking smack about my mom, in my mom's own home, to a new employee on the day my dad died and Mom lost her husband of forty-five-and-a-half years, Sharon became a full-blown-brat-child-bitch. After Katie left, I asked Sharon to please call or dial for me on my phone, Mary, so I could tell her about Dad. I didn't want to wait until the next day, My Mary Tuesday, actually what was going to be our Friendsgiving, and have her walk into a mopey, sad, funky day without warning, especially since it was planned that we were going to call Mary before anyone else.

Sharon flat-ass refused to do as I asked like she had the authority to deny me my request and access to my phone. This was my first "pick your battle" moment with her. This is how the conversation went down:

Me: I know you two don't care for each other for whatever reason, but I don't care about that right now. Would you please call Mary for me on my phone so I can tell her that Dad has gone to Hawaii.

Sharon: No, why would I do that?

Me: Because I just asked you to.

Sharon: You're not ready to do this. You have to process what has happened today.

Me: Excuse me? I am processing what has happened today, and calling Mary is part of my process.

Sharon: I still don't think you are ready, and I'm not going to do it.

Me: So you want me to make my mom call Susan (Sharon's boss) on the day my dad dies and tell her that you are not doing what I asked you to do?

Sharon: I dare you. It will be your word against mine.

Now being really upset and pissed, I did something I should not have done. It was pretty classless. I threatened her job.

Me: I can make it so you don't have a job in five minutes.

Sharon: Who do you think you are?

Me: Your one and only Fucking client! So, I suggest you dial Mary's number, now.

She did and didn't say another word. She didn't help me with the call other than dial and put the phone on speaker. Mary did offer to come right over, which I knew she would, but I told her that I was okay and be ready for our Friendsgiving tomorrow because I was going to need laughing, distractions and some of her dancing.

After the phone call ended, and waiting for the blow-back for speaking my mind and taking ownership of my . . .I don't even know what to call it . . .self, life, direction, control, mental-health, strength . . .all of it, I ran with the feeling and announced, **and announced**, that I wanted a

McDonald's fish-fillet meal and that Sharon needed to order it through DoorDash now. All she said was okay. She didn't even try and talk me into pizza like every other day. After that, our whole conversation and phone call was swept under the rug and never talked about again, that is, until many months later, when I finally remembered the incident and shared it with my mom and actually also with Mary at the same time.

***

The next day, Mary and I did have our Friendsgiving. Weeks before I had also extended an invitation to Sharon to join us, which she declined because she didn't like Mary and didn't want to be around us together. The weird thing is . . .guess who showed up, busting right into the house without knocking like she owned the place (just like she did every day she worked, until my mom started locking the door which royally pissed Sharon off and forced her to knock)? Mary and I had the music blasting, the cookies baking, the "adult" eggnog flowing when we were shocked into silence. We stared at each other with a WTF look on our faces. Sharon not only re-invited herself but showed up empty-handed and helped herself to our booze without an invite.

At that exact moment, Mom had come inside from the garage for some reason and witnessed the goings-on. (She had been separating-out my dad's things.) She was privy to the whole Sharon and Mary not-liking-each-other situation. The look on her face could only be described, as was ours, as a WTF stare.

We never did figure out why Sharon decided to crash our party. It was never talked about, just like the "I could get you fired in five minutes" phone call was never mentioned . . .actually, just like the next comment Mary made as she left that day was never discussed: "It's okay. I'll be here way more often, anyway," which Mom not only didn't understand but totally missed . . .at least for a few months until she finally got the meaning of Mary's last jab at Sharon.

I really didn't know how soon that was going to happen, Mary being here more often. As it turned out, it occurred sooner than I expected.

***

It was only a couple of weeks later that Katie came to work as a fill-in for Sharon and let the cat out of the bag. She waited until almost the end of the day before she said anything. I'm guessing that since she hadn't met my mom yet she was waiting and saving judgement on her.

When she finally fessed-up about the interaction between herself and Sharon, she said, "Ya, I wasn't going to acknowledge that kind of comment, so I played the deaf card. I didn't respond to Sharon. I acted my part, deaf. I knew I'd form my own opinion once I met your mom."

Then Katie repeated—verbatim, to both my mom and me—what Sharon had said about always having to walk on egg-shells around my mom, which is exactly what I heard from the bathroom that day and which was the same damn thing she said to me after the whole email debacle— something she denied saying up until the last day we ever spoke—when she couldn't resign my mom back into my mom's own email account.

Don't get me wrong. Like my mom has always said, Sharon came at exactly the right time in my family's life when Mom needed someone to basically run the household in her absence. So, I must digress. I'm not saying it was all bad with Sharon. We had our fun times, too . . .in the beginning, for sure. The disconnect occurred when I came into my power, noticing and understanding that I was not being heard, that I was being disrespected and that I was feeling like I was being owned.

After that strange Friendsgiving interaction, and because Mom was home and no longer spending all of her days with my dad at the assisted-living facility, I didn't have to tattle anymore or question the things that were being done and going on. I didn't have to run my questions and concerns by Mary, my sounding board. Mom began to see and experience them for herself. And, she began to push back, hard, to regain the ownership of her own home that Sharon didn't want to give back and pretty much fought to keep a hold on, asking things like "Are we going to have a problem with (fill in the blank), too?" To which my mom would answer "No, not as long as it is done my way in my home."

Those were the weird control kinds of things that were going on, not to mention the lack of respect shown by Sharon for **my mother's** house . . .her home and everything in it, including her daughter. (Sorry, I had to put that in there.) To put it in perspective, yes, mom was grateful that Sharon had stepped in to hold down the fort, but now that she was back full-time in her own home, Sharon didn't want to relinquish control or ownership of the house back to its rightful owner: Mom.

Just as an example, and, like I mentioned earlier, I have a giant wall in my bedroom covered in photos. I use a variety of hanging devices: nails, command hooks, command tape, etc. One day when removing one of the photo frames attached with command tape from the wall, Sharon didn't know how to properly remove the tape without taking off the paint and ripping off the dry wall. And that is exactly what happened. I immediately groaned, "Oh, crap! Mom is not going to be happy."

To which Sharon shrugged and said, "Oh, well, no biggy. Why do we even have to tell her?"

All I could think was, "Oh, My God, Oh, My God! She is so gonna find out and be sooooo mad."

And she was! It didn't take much for Mom to notice the hole in the wall, although it did take a day. And she did come unglued. And Sharon heard about it that same day.

Mom asked her what the hell happened, even though she already knew, and why she didn't tell Mom about it when it happened. Sharon sheepishly admitted that she didn't know how to remove the tape, never having used it before, then condescendingly commented, "It's no big deal."

My red mama, Mitzi, came out: "First of all, if you don't know how to do something, don't do it. Secondly, what would you do if one of your kids ripped a hole in your wall, didn't tell you about it and tried to hide it?"

"Well, well, well, wel . . .I wouldn't be happy," was all Sharon could come-up with as an answer.

***

Needless to say, the following month after my dad died, my mother and I went through a lot of "stuff" . . .I'm talking emotional stuff, for sure, but also stuff like making changes to bills and other paperwork, like wills and such, making phone calls to family and friends, physically packing up all of his belongings and deciding what went where and to whom, dealing with the "gone-ness" of him and the overwhelmingness of it all.

A few days before Christmas, while navigating our new reality, Mom and I had a conversation that I didn't know at the time would alter Life, life as I had known it for the past eight months, anyway. We sat down over coffee and probably my brownie, if I remember correctly, and talked about how things had changed so much and how much was still going to change. Mom talked about how she had been spending so much time with Dad and away from home and feeling like she needed to be more aware of what was going on with me first-hand, at the moment it happened, and how she needed to gain back control of her own environment—her home, what she did with her time, who she saw and when, etc. She said that she felt like she needed time . . .like time without people . . .just a little . . .just me and her time.

At first, I was a bit taken-aback, not understanding what was going on in her head. Mine is complicated enough without trying to get into someone else's. But after thinking about it for a couple of minutes, I did understand. I sort of felt the same. We needed space to do whatever the hell we wanted or needed to do . . .without other people, without judgment or suggestions as to what we should or shouldn't be doing or feeling or thinking getting in our way.

Mom let me know that she had made a decision to cut back from having a care-provider here five days a week to four days a week to give us, me and her, a time for remembering, for doing nothing, for doing everything, for de-stressing, for doing whatever the fuck we wanted to do day during the middle of the week . . .a break from, I don't know, the outside world.

We discussed the fact that it was the holiday season and we, neither of us, wanted to change things for anyone until after the first of the year. Remember, we had one person, Sharon, four days a week and one person, Mary, one day a week, so it was kind of a no-brainer for us who was going to get cut a day, at least for a while. And that decision was greatly influenced by what was going on daily between Sharon and Mom. Still Mom thought she was being thoughtful waiting until after the holidays to make the change because how unkind and unfair is it to cut someone's hours right before Christmas. At the end of our conversation, I did ask Mom if it was okay that I gave Sharon a "heads-up" as to what was going to happen at the first of the year. Mom said, "If you feel the need to give Sharon a heads-up, go ahead. It is probably the right thing to do."

Boy did that back-fire!

On the morning of December 21, 2023, a Wednesday, after asking for weeks to walk to CVS to get pictures printed, Sharon and I were leaving the store and standing in the parking lot when I told her that Mom (or Mom and I, I can't remember which; I think I have a mental block about what exactly went down) decided to drop a day, at least for a while, of home-care for me and explained why. Her response was, "Why are you waiting until January?"

I explained to Sharon that we didn't want to leave anyone hanging, cutting a paycheck for them, and causing stress over the holidays. I said "anyone" because I never specifically said that it was she who was going to have time cut. She just assumed, I guess (but rightfully so, because it *was* going to be her). To be honest, even though we hadn't formally talked to either Sharon or Mary about the change in schedule, they both seemed to have a premonition, a hunch, that things were going to proceed differently than they had.

I know Mary was hoping that Sharon would quit, because she had previously said it out loud. (Things usually happen when they are said out loud.) Mary was ready to jump in full-time. And because Sharon and Mom were butting heads so much, my mom was pretty sure Sharon had been trying to figure out how to quit for a while and save face at the same time. That was sort of our hope, our plan: that Sharon would opt to leave instead of take a cut in time and pay . . .but not right away, not within five minutes of my little heads-up conversation.

We, my mom and I, seemed to have fallen right into Sharon's wily ruse. Like (how does that saying go?), like-white-on-rice, Sharon, in seconds, brazenly and unapologetically, while walking behind me, smoking and on her phone, not paying any attention to me, was texting Mary to see if she could finish out the week because today was her last day.

I full-on panicked! I spent the entire walk home asking myself WTF did I just do? Mom is going to kill me. I just put a bump in a road that was supposed to go along smoothly. I thought I was being nice by giving Sharon a heads-up, but, instead, Sharon bit me in the butt by quitting on the spot. I really felt like it was more of a Fuck You move on her part.

By the time Sharon and I got home, Mary had copied and pasted the texts from Sharon and sent them to my mom and asked, "What the hell is going on?!" This was the exact text that Mary forwarded to my mom:

Sharon: I'm going to be stepping away from work. Can you fill in the rest of the week? You can contact Mitzi or Jenni later on this afternoon to discuss the future plans with them.

Mary: No, I have things going on this week. Are you all right?

Sharon: Yes, I'm ok but it's time you help with their healing process because I'm a constant reminder of the lose [loss] they just had and it's hard on Mitzi. You bring silliness and joy when you're around. That's what they need right now, and not someone who is sad and emotional.

To which my mom answered, "I have no clue. I just drove up into the driveway. I'll let you know when I as I know."

As soon as my mom walked through the door, Sharon stated, "We need to talk." And bless her heart, Mom acted like she was clueless as to anything going on.

Sharon laid out the conversation she and I had had over the last hour and what she had decided, deleting the fact that she had asked me if I liked Mary better than her. I know I've mentioned that tidbit of information before but, really? I can't get over her asking me that. Who, I mean what adult, asks that kind of question? She had already told me, in the middle of the CVS parking lot that today was going to be her last day. I don't know; I could be wrong; I don't think I am, though. It seemed really odd how quickly Sharon was able to come up with a plan of what "we" were going to tell people why she left, and, interestingly, it had nothing to do with us cutting a day. That aspect was never mentioned by her.

The story she presented in short was something like this:

I've decided that I need to spend time with my family. (Her husband also had cancer, something we were not supposed to know: another rule broken.) Since Doug has passed away, it has been hard for me to be around you guys. It is too sad. I need to get through my shit and you need to heal from yours. We'll tell everybody that it was a mutual thing.

Well, it only took a short time until I called BULLS**** on that story. The more I thought about it, in my opinion, it was her attempt to "cover her ass" with a made-up excuse that she expected my mom and me to go along with and verbally vomit when asked. It wasn't more than a week before one of the care-coordinators asked what the real story was, and my mom and I were more than happy to share. She is no longer a care-provider.

At first, Mary became my four-day-a-week person, since Mom and I were taking *our-day* during the middle of the week. Now Mary is with me five days a week, and I haven't had pizza for months.

***

As sort of a little side note, and for shits and giggles, I'd like to share here a few of the other care-providers I had while Sharon or Mary were unable to make a shift due to illness, appointments, vacations or whatever. Sometimes they were very good, and sometimes they were their own circus show . . .or better explained . . . shit show.

Who should I start with . . . hmmm . . .I think Micheal. Please remember that I am at present a forty-five-year-old female who needs to have my ass wiped. That entails being basically undressed from the waist down by another human being while hanging from the ceiling of my bedroom with said-butt at about the level of a care-givers face. Now if that isn't awkward enough, for both me and the care-giver, imagine how I felt when I watched a man walk up to our front-door with his Partners In Care name tag on. 'HELL TO THE NO!' That was the first thing that came out of my mouth.

Reality check here: do I really need to spell this out? The last date/no-date I had was in my senior year of high school with one of my friends. Neither one of us had a date (nor had I ever had one), so we sort of just went together. We both wanted to dress-up and go to the homecoming dance. There was no hand-holding, no kissing or any other kind of contact, other than that of friendship. What I'm getting at is that I'm not only a forty-five-year-old virgin, I'm a forty-five-

year-old never-been-touched-in-that-way . .
.ever . . .person. Are you getting my drift? It
isn't like I didn't or don't know about sex. I
do. I've been around animals my whole life. I
actually raised and bred sheep for years and
know all about how that works. I just haven't
experienced it myself.

So, back to Micheal. Nope. I was so not
comfortable meeting him for the first time
and then, thirty minutes later, having him
drop my pants and get up close and personal.

The funny thing was, he didn't realize
I was a female until he got here, nor did he
understand why he was sent to care for a
female, never having cared for a female
before. I guess it is done, but we both
thought we each should have been made
aware and asked if we were okay with the
set-up.

The three of us visited for a bit on the
porch, laughing at the situation. I remember
my mom telling Micheal that he was

probably a very nice guy, but that no matter how nice and adept at his job he was, this was probably not going to be a good fit.

***

Next up: a woman named Wanda. Wanda, Wanda, Wanda . . .Now, I'm not one to judge a person or a person's looks. I mean I'm in no position to judge anyone for anything, but OH MY GOD! This woman walked into our house and filled every breathable speck of air with the smell of overpowering old-lady perfume, ya know, like Wind Song, and cigarettes. It was truly gag-worthy. Then she said something about being fifty-five, but she looked way older than my mom who was seventy at the time. The term 'rode hard and put up wet' was thrown around after she left. She also wore a very long blonde wig that was not, shall I say, the best quality. She said she wore it because she had something called alopecia. This will be important later. I mean, she was nice enough, but she did some pretty bizarre things. She read to me from my own book, *Little Diva On Wheels,* like I didn't know what I wrote.

Now this is gross, ya'll. Not that I really should or want to share this, but if I was throwing flags, this would have been, not red flag number four, but fluorescent-red-danger-road-pylon number four. As with Micheal, what I'm trying to get you to understand (as someone who may need help from an outside source) is that you can pick and choose who you let into your home . . .for whatever reason: be it personality differences, work-ethics or even, and especially, as in Wanda's case, health and safety issues.

Let me explain. Sometime during the day Wanda had shared, among other issues, that she had a leakage problem. TMI, I know. It was for me, too. After she had left for the day, we found in my bathroom, on the shelf below the mirror, a sanitary napkin soaked with urine. I wanted to vomit!!!! It wasn't in the garbage or even wrapped in toilet paper. It was just lying there in open, plain view. But that was not the worst Wanda offense.

Remember that she had shared that she wore a wig because of her skin condition? Well, she spent a good part of the day scratching, more like digging -at, her head through the wig. After the fact, my mom said that she had noticed little blotches of blood on one of Wanda's fingers and had mentioned it to her. Wanda blew it off, and Mom forgot about it. Mom forgot about it until she went to take me to the bathroom and found blood on everything I owned, from my wheelchair, to my sling, to my lift, to the belt that holds me into my wheelchair, to the waist of my pants, and every other thing she touched. At that point my mom wanted to vomit!

Mom immediately did two things. She called Partner's In Care and told them about our, shall I call it, experience with Wanda and in no uncertain terms told them that Wanda would never be allowed into our house, ever. The second thing she did was wash, disinfect and sanitize everything in the whole house. If she could have put my bed in the washing machine, she would have. And although my dad didn't interact with Wanda at all (and he never said anything bad about any of my care-givers, before or after Wanda), he gimped his way out of his bedroom and stated (he didn't ask), "She's not coming back."

Mom: "It's been taken care of."

***

Those were the two most notable, but there were other still unacceptable (although less traumatic and horrifying) care-providers who were dispatched to my home to assist me with my needs.

One was a woman who came in, sat down on the sofa and asked, "Do you want to watch TV?," like it, the TV, was going to be my babysitter for the day. She was pleasant enough and had no problem feeding me or taking me to the bathroom, when needed, but she was really put out if I asked her to do any of the household chores I had taken on over the last few months.

That might need some explaining . . .me and household chores, that is. Considering as a quadriplegic I physically can't perform any household task by myself, it doesn't fit the puzzle. The thing is, since it is now just my mom and me in the home and since we each have six hours to ourselves, by ourselves apart from each other, I took it upon myself to help, to participate in the upkeep of our home . . .with the help of my hired hands. I have to admit, it felt a little weird in the beginning, taking control of anything in the house I lived in. My parents always did everything. I mean, as kids, my siblings and I all had chores to do. Mine were mostly made up, though. My mom would tie a wet rag around my hand and have me wash door jams and such. She did the same with a dust rag to dust what I could reach. It was also my job to check through the whole house, or the rooms I could navigate to and through, to find dirty dishes and report back to where they were to my mom.

(In writing this I just now found out she planted them there in the first place.)

Aaaaaa . . .back in the day.

Anyway, another less than ideal woman, who showed up one day, did just that. She showed up. She spent her time sitting at the kitchen island playing with her phone, drinking from her water bottle continually, filling it with ice and water from the refrigerator and therefore spending an equal amount of time in the bathroom, if you get my drift, and snacking from her seemingly never-empty bag. But yet she never offered me lunch or asked if I was hungry. It wasn't until my mom came in the house from working on a pottery order and asked me if I had had lunch yet that I was actually fed . . .BY MY MOM. And, and, and, like I mentioned, every time I had to pee, she had to pee first! It could have really been a problem for me if I had been in a hurry.

***

If you have learned anything about me at all reading through these pages, you have figured out that I am a visitor. I am a nosy busybody who wants to know everything a person is willing to share with me. Simply stated, I can be a nosy bitch, if I choose to be. I suppose it is my way of living vicariously through other people's lives and experiences, experiences I am either not likely to experience myself or would like to experience for myself. I'm basically gathering an inventory of ideas and prior knowledge that an able-bodied person would already possess but that is foreign to me or that I have an understanding-of or an understanding that I could possibly do . . .or not.

So, with the two "less than ideal" women just mentioned, there no real memorable interaction or conversation between us. I learned nothing from them that I can to this day remember. They gave me not one iota of information to help fill my library of, as my mom would call it, "we'll give it a shot" list or even a jeopardy answer. I mean, come on . . .I don't know everything. Make me stretch my brain or something. Make me wonder or ponder something, anything. Give me something to question or judge or compare my life to. Give me ideas about normalcy, not just any normalcy, but your normalcy, and let me share mine with you. We may not be that far apart . . .

Needless to say, Mary and I were on the phone the following Monday morning to add said-women onto my no-go list, the list that seems to keep growing.

On the other side of the no-go list were or are the women who belong on the yes-please list. One such woman is Katie, who I have mentioned before. Although she was legally deaf (she could hear a little), Katie and I still had days full of conversations while completing my self-imposed household chores. I mean, I even know now that there is a linguistic issue due-to or because-of deafness. For example, Katie can't stand to have to say the word "purple" because she knows she pronounces it incorrectly Every. Single. Damn. Time., she complained to me while sharing our defuncts or the obstacles we both have to conquer: or at least work on. She says she knows that she says it wrong, but there is something about the *u-r* combination that is weirdly a linguistically difficult, almost impossible sound for her to make. Who knew? . . . not me, but I loved to get her to have to use the word purple every chance I got, all in good fun, with her acceptance, of course. It helps that my favorite color is purple. And we laughed. I, of course, shared that I have difficulty with multiple words because of my own speech pattern, my CP babbleistics, as I call it.

Another couple of women whom I have had over the last couple of years as fill-in care-givers are Rene and Leah. Both ladies, although from way different age groups and generations (I could be Rene's mother, and Leah could be mine; we did the math), more than treated me as an intelligent, thinking, interesting person, equal to them in every way. They, like all of the yes-please folks on my list, have and continue to show genuine interest in me, my condition, my life and my history. I'm not just a let's turn on the television babysitting job for them. In fact, I probably have learned and know as much about them through our gossip-visiting sessions as they know about me. I'm not just talking about Rene and Leah here but all of the "keepers" as I call them. We have become not just client and care-giver but friends, as well, keeping each other abreast of what is going on in each of our lives . . .from boyfriends to babies. I love running into any and all of any one of them while out and about with my mom or more usually with "My Mary."

I've already talked about Mary, pretty in-depth actually. Although all of my other "keeper" care-givers are great, respectful and interested in me and all, Mary has always been intriguingly, almost obsessively, interested in not only me and my life but, more so, in about what I thought and what I had to say. (I don't know why I said thought instead of think. She still does.) When she first started, Mary wanted to know about all of my experiences, the ones I've had and the ones I haven't had. And the ones I haven't had, Mary was going to make damn sure I had them. She was curious about why I was disabled and how I do 'stuff' as a differently-abled person. I tell you what, she dug deep, sometimes invasively deep. I know it sounds like I mean that in a bad way, but I don't. I mean it in the best way, ever.

This reminds me of a short story I want to share to explain what I mean.

Years ago, when I was about two-years-old, my mom, dad and I went on vacation and visit extended family in Kentucky. It is my understanding that it was really, really hot, and from day one, I have never done well in the heat. Because of that, and because air-conditioning is sort of nonexistent back there, we, all us women folk (that's truly what they say back there), took a trip to the local Piggly Wiggly, a place where they run air-conditioning freely. Yes, they do exist!

Anyway, as I was relishing in the coolness,

flopped loosely in my ugly semi-wheelchair, a woman walked up to my mother and asked point blank, "What's wrong with that baby?!" (Insert deep Southern, super-inquisitive accent and unabashed boldness.)

As the story goes, my mother was extremely shocked at the woman's brazen approach and couldn't answer. Step in my great-grandmother to handle the situation, telling the woman, "There ain't nothing wrong with this baby! She's just relaxin'. You should see her play the organ!" Situation handled. Woman walks away happy with the answer. Everyone satisfied. Except maybe my mom, for a minute.

Her recollection was more like "How dare she walk up and ask me that! Wait, that was kind of refreshing. Instead of staring or playing the look-but-don't-look game, she actually came up and asked, kind of like a kid would do." (Hence, the topic of learned behavior that I brought up in a previous volume of my autobiography.)

The point here is, there is a . . .cultural . . .I guess you'd call it . . .difference between

California's West Coast attitudes, a stiffness, maybe, and Kentucky's Southern,   friendly, informal attitude about what is and isn't . . .I don't know . . .acceptable behavior and acceptance itself.

Mary is not only my appreciated Kentucky, inquisitive, in your face woman, but also my Kentucky great-grandmother who is going to stand up to others, as well as stand up for me.

***

In previous volumes of my books, *Little Diva On Wheels* and *Even Broken-Winged Divas Can Fly*, I talk about the "we'll give it a shot" attitude my parents, especially my mother, had with me growing-up and experiencing and being exposed to all that I could be. But it had, and has always been from a mother's perspective, things a mother would think was important or worthwhile to life fulfilling blah, blah, blah . . .I mean, there are some things a mother wouldn't even consider exposing her kid, even an adult kid, as I am, a daughter, to. For sure, it has nothing to do with being disabled and everything to do with a parental mindset.

Take a second and, as a parent, think about what I might be talking about here. Those "other things" just wouldn't cross a mother's or father's, for that matter, mind. But I found out, with the right person, that there is so much more to experience than the mother blah, blah, blah. Those things, for sure, are girlfriend topics. The things I have done and talked about with Mary are from that girlfriend place. It is all from a peer point of view, not from a parental point of view, mostly.

Actually, to begin with, Mary and I, like every other new person who steps into my life, were on a slow kind of roll getting to know each other . . .for like a day and a half. Besides learning the ropes, the how-to-dos of feeding and bath-rooming and such, Mary was, in those first days (now very surprising to me and absolutely opposite to who she is with me now), fairly quiet and subdued. She listened, asked questions, called my dad Mr. Kuhns instead of Doug, and shared her past experiences as a care-provider with my mom, my dad and me.

Again, initially, she was only here one day a week, and you would have thought it would have taken us longer than it did, the two Tuesdays, to become so comfortable with each other. In the short time it took for us to get to know each other, Mary was never my boss, nor ever my babysitter, but my equal; I am her equal. And during my time with care-providers, I have been both: the babysat, and bossed.

Speaking of equal, I remember the first time the three of us, my mom, Mary and I, went shopping together at Walmart. We were looking for something to go over my arm-lateral-pad-supports that could be removed and washed. Summertime in Chico gets hot and therefore pretty stinky. Anyway, I remember my mom pushing the cart and doing a little swaying and bopping to the store music. I was mortified by her, albeit discreet and slight, dance moves in the store . . . in public. It wasn't until Mom and I looked to our right and saw Mary in her full-arm swivel, hip-swinging, head-banging, OMG life-loving dance in that store, absolutely in public, that I realized that "My Mary" was going to take over where my parents had brought me to thus far. I also realized that I was totally okay with Mary's getting jiggy-with-it dance because it is who she is. I recognized that day, I admit, that I may have been a little up-tight until that point, a bit stiff in my own being, and that I needed to give myself and my mom, for another, permission to sway, bop and jig, yes, even in public.

I must give kudos to my parents for raising me with manners and politeness and not giving me a pass in life because I am disabled. My mother, from day one, has always told me, "You are already different and weird to other people: Don't give them a reason to look down on you, too. Be respectful. Please and Thank-you goes a long way." So I guess that translates/translated to me as always acting prim and proper when in public, so that my mother's swaying to the music was a less-than-ideal behavior in my mind, especially for a mother, for *my* mother. Mary kicked that mindset in the butt. Now we dance in public all the time, even with my mother.

Mary not only accidently loosened my uptight nature; she made it her mission to change the way I spoke or approached or answered people. In her mind, I was her boss. It infuriated her that I would ask for something, instead of telling her what to do or what I wanted, something as simple as getting my keys out of my bag for the mailbox or making me coffee. I've always <u>asked</u> people to do things for me. *"Would you make me a cup of coffee, please?"* or *"Would you get my keys out of my bag so we can get the mail, please?"*

Mary continually, gently reminded me that I was her boss, that she was here to work and do for me, do what I needed or wanted, not what she wanted to do. Mary enlightened me to the fact, as she saw it, that asking gives her or anyone else the option of saying "No."

Interestingly enough, I do recall, as you may remember, the days of Sharon and her foot issue, her back issue and, especially, on the day my dad passed, her not wanting to call Mary as I asked her to do. She had no trouble telling me that she was going to sit on her ass (my words, not her's) and saying "No" to anything I proposed doing those days. (I mean, why come to work if your foot or back hurts so bad that you can't walk, move or perform your outlined duties?)

Another lesson Mary insisted on teaching me was "Stop saying okay" or "I'm okay" to every and all things: the word okay is like a blanket non-response response or an okay-whatever response . . .like "Go ahead and do whatever it is you want to do," which may or may not really be okay with you and also allows people to take advantage of you. She suggested (and I have noticed since she brought it up) that people respond differently when I respond with "I'm good" or "I hear you" rather than with "I'm okay" or "It's okay." I've learned that I get more of an interactive response with "I hear you, but I'd rather . . ." or "I'm good with that for lunch, but I'd like orange soda, too, please." These are seemingly small things, small words, small changes, but they make an immense difference in the life of someone who depends on others for every little thing . . ., maybe placing a little more power in that dependent person's hands. And, as my mother says, you can still be polite and have manners while you are being the boss. Although, Mary is still dying to hear me call her a BITCH . . .for any reason. I have told her that I am saving that for a very big and special reason, maybe an emergency, just to make sure she hears me.

Even though Mary has been a care-provider for many years, hanging with me has opened her eyes to the world around "me," a world that can be very rude, but we'll get to that in a bit. It wasn't until we were able to spend the days by ourselves without my mom that Mary realized just how rude. In the beginning, my mom would drop us off at the mall, and then we would call her hours later when we were ready to come home, or more likely than not, Mom would call me and say, "Hey, Mary needs to head home in thirty minutes. I need to come get you guys." And so it went . . .for a while.

***

It took us close to a year before my mom felt comfortable and confident enough that Mary felt comfortable and confident enough for Mary to drive our giant size van that we call the BUS and go out by ourselves. Mary had been loading me into the van and doing the tie-downs almost from the beginning, since the very first time the three of us went out. There were occasions, though, when she would step back and let my mom do it because she got my wheelchair sideways or stuck, throwing her hands in the air saying, "You do it. I give up." But once Mary was loading and unloading me like pro, Mom decided, although frightfully and dubiously, that we were good to go.

Actually, even though Mary had to have her own car insurance to work for Partners In Care and possibly drive for a client, Mom, on the QT, added Mary to her car insurance as a driver on the van. The funny thing is, Mom didn't mention that news to either Mary or me until a couple of weeks after the fact. I guess she was still grappling with the idea of me going out by myself . . .not by myself, but by myself without her. I'm sure I've mentioned at least a multitude of times that my mom and I have always pretty much been attached at the hip. As she later explained it, she was truly fearful and unsettled with putting her trust of me, my life, my well-being, totally in someone else's hands other than her own, so much so that she had to 'sneak-up' on the idea herself before she finally was able to tell us that we could venture out on our own . . .by ourselves, leaving her at home stewing in her pot of anxiety, distress and trepidation.

Mom's only saving grace was that Mary understood her mind-set and nervousness. I mean, Mary is a mom, too, with a teenage boy graduating from high-school, ready to move out and be on his own. The difference between the two mothers is that Mary has had time and experiences working up to her kid being and living independently. In my forty-five years on this earth, I can probably count on one hand how many times, days or nights my mom hasn't been with me—two babies after me, a couple of business trips to San Francisco and the day she had her angioplasty—and then I was either home with my dad or other family members, not, as she would now jokingly say, roaming the streets.

Besides that, Mary was insightful enough to understand my mom's uneasiness. There is this thing, this app, that you can put on your phone called 'Life 360,' which Mary put on both mine and my mother's phones. It basically tracks where you are, how long you have been where you are, how fast you are going, if you are driving or walking, and if you have been in an accident. Luckily, she has never seen that pop-up on her phone, nor have I. It turns out I need the app as much as she does; I get freaked out when she leaves home and I don't know it, even if I'm out and about in town. Who knew I had the same attachment issues . . .lol.

Us, Mary and me, going out by ourselves was only one of the first 'FIRSTS' we have experienced. Besides giving me a way bigger voice than I have ever had, Mary has introduced me to fun with freedom and independence. When I say freedom, I'm not only talking freedom from being confined or having someone continually by my side or being guided or overseen but a renewed freedom of movement that I hadn't realized I had lost.

When I was a kid I remember when I got my first electric wheelchair and sitting in the middle of the driveway with the joystick jammed to one side or the other, on purpose, and spinning until I made myself dizzy; then I'd go the other way.

One of the first things Mary suggested we do was to go roller skating. I remember looking at her like she was absolutely crazy. Turns out, her son works at the local skating rink and she was able to confirm with him that, for sure, I could skate. The rink not only has people in wheelchairs 'skate,' if you will, but the place has PVC pipe rolling-walkers for little kids, or even big kids, just learning to skate.

I turned up my chair to the highest speed setting and took off. Oh My God! The feeling of freedom was epic! I felt like I was like in a movie with the wind blowing through my hair as I ran across the ~~rink~~ field trying to keep up with Mary. The only thing that I had to remember was to go in the same direction as all of the other skaters. That was the only rule I had to follow, the only confining element, and I was totally digging it!

The next big thing we did (I get skating wouldn't be a big thing for most people, but it was for me), I instigated. One day after Mary had left, I saw an advertisement on TV about "The Hunks," a touring all-male revue show. I didn't really know what a revue show was, and I figured it probably wasn't something I wanted to discuss with my mother, just seeing the mostly naked guys on the poster. So the following day I had Mary sit down at the computer with me and check out exactly what and who they were. Well, it turns out The Hunks are a group of a dozen or so guys, sort of exotic dancers, all cute and very well built, in my opinion, who put on a pretty provocative show. I proposed to Mary that we go. She was so on-board.

But as Mary and I began to chat about a second "First" for me, we realized the possibility of there being a slight problem. The show was an evening affair and an hour away. Even though we had van-driving privileges around town, we both comprehended the difference for my mom between day-and-night and in-town and out-of-town driving excursions by Mary and me, not only knowing but also understanding that Mom was not going to go for a night-time outing an hour away.

Earlier on in my writing I said something about—those "other things" that just wouldn't cross a mother's or father's mind. Well, here is me bringing up to my mother's mind the idea of going to a show to watch naked guys dance. I still remember the bewildered look on her face as she tried to digest the words I had just spoken to her.

"A what? When? Wha . . .? Where? What are you talking about? Oh . . .like exotic dancers? OMG! Are you kidding. And, and, and . . .you want me to go?"

I was on top of it. "Well, actually, we figured it boiled down to the fact that you'd most likely not be okay with us going by ourselves but that you might be open and willing to go with us so you could drive."

"Someone has done their homework," my mother sputtered.

"When have I ever not?"

"Okay, then, tell me about this whole thing."

During my mother's and my exchange, I noticed Mary sitting quietly to the side, smiling like the Cheshire Cat. Later, when we were alone, online, ordering three tickets that I proudly paid for, Mary commented on my newly developing voice and that this was going to be another "First."

The reality of the whole thing is that it was a litany of firsts, not just for me, but for all three of us. I was going to see my first naked guy show. Mom was going to see her first naked guy show. We were going to see our first naked guy show together—one of those not talked about mother-daughter topics. Mary, for the first time ever, was going with a mother-daughter duo to a naked guy show. It could have all been very awkward, but for some reason, it wasn't— even when my mom was helping me shove dollar-bills down multiple guys' pants. And this is going to sound most unbelievable and uncharacteristic, but when I was getting a lap dance from a couple of the guys, they were so very respectful and even thoughtful and gentle, no doubt because of my purple accessory, my wheelchair, but they also treated me like I was a full-fledged paying customer. In the words of John Rich, *Save a horse. Ride a cowboy.* Woo Hoo!

***

Obviously, seeing mostly naked guys dance was definitely a first for me and maybe a little traumatic for my mom. But with my dad passing away and Mary joining us in our home full-time, I have had a huge number of firsts, mostly good, some not so good.

The good-firsts range from ax throwing, yup with real axes, to spending the entire day at the mall shopping or dressing up as a unicorn (as I call myself) for Halloween and hitting-up all the local bars in town with Mary to, not drink, necessarily, but hang and enjoy people and the surroundings . . .Mary called it eye-candy, and I found out that I really like candy.

Then there are the need-to-know firsts, the learning experiences, like the realization that I need to wait and have my Starbucks coffee and brownie at the end of our outings instead of at the beginning. Who knew I almost immediately need to rush home and relieve myself until the first time I didn't make it home to use the facilities. I now understand this was something my mom had always choreographed into our, hers and my, daily-outings. When I asked her about it, she said that she learned early on that coffee and I are not really that compatible. And life is all about the timing.

The not-so-good-firsts pretty much all have to do with M-O-N-E-Y. Money really kind of sucks . . .the not having it or having to pay attention to if you do or don't have enough of it . . .and then there is how to or not to spend it.

I've always been, in a blasé kind of way, aware of my finances. (I actually hate numbers!) And my mother has always, not managed my money, but overseen and maybe made suggestions on if I could or couldn't afford something or really, really needed it or really, or really, really wanted it, making me think, as she says, "long and hard about it." I do have bills that I have taken responsibility for like my cell-phone bill, the internet bill, the land-line (mostly for my own emergency use with a touch-pad) and of course my portion of the shared Mastercard bill. (Just as an FYI, my mom and I share a credit card, PayPal account, Amazon account and wherever else we shop account, just because it makes life easier for her: not so many cards, in-coming bills to keep track of, etc.).

The down-side of becoming my new independent-self is that I didn't think I had a mother-buffer when I was out doing my adult-thing. Mary will never tell me how to or not to spend my money. She has told me numerous times that that is not her job. I was under the very false impression (given by a less than spontaneous spender, my mother) that I had been given full-rein of my checkbook and credit/debit card with virtually no over-sight. Because of that train of thought, I financially fell on my face, big time, but just once, so far. I got down to a very spooky $3.00 to my name. I'm talking not even coffee-cup-holder change in the van.

As I began spending like a stupid person, I believed that I had no one's thumb holding me down or watching what I was doing, money-wise. I was so fucking wrong.

My mom was watching, invisibly wiggling her thumb just above and behind my puffed-up ego and planning for what was to be my first epic adulting-fail. She did what she always does. She gave me enough rope to hang myself, setting me up for a reality check.

Even though we both have online banking nowadays, my mother, I'm sure, opted for dramatics, presented me with a paper-printout of my bank balance. I panicked. Then, as if she knew this was going to happen, Mom pulled out a small spiral notebook already filled out with my income and expenditures on the first page. I was stunned, not so much because I was down to three dollars (I actually wasn't immediately aware of it), but more so because my mom knew almost the minute it happened and was prepared with one of those lectures . . .ya know, one of those, if you are going to spend money like you have no sense or bills, let's break down what it costs to be an adult.

Man, adulting is expensive and maybe over-rated . . .; forget maybe; it is freaking over-rated. Yes, I have van-access privileges with the van that my mother bought, but now I have to pay for my own gas when I use it. Since I use the van with Mary more than I use it with my mother, I have to pick up half the insurance and half of the van maintenance. We also discussed and implemented the concept of sharing the grocery bill and contributing to our crock-pot petty cash fund for the house. All that play money that I used to have, I don't have anymore, because I want and have been given freedom, away and separate from my mom and as an individual, and . . .What is that song? . . .*Freedom isn't free*.

After I picked my jaw up off the floor, and after being freaked and embarrassed, returned to my former child-self, Mom and I went over the numbers and the responsibilities of being the adult I thought I was. As I said before, Mom has always guided me or suggested how to spend, save or just 'use' my money.

Before the whole 'what happens to me when both of my parents are gone' issue was finally confronted and addressed, I absolutely knew, understood, realized and appreciated the fact that they, my parents, paid for most everything I did, have, ate, drank, played with, wore . . .you get the picture. The minimal amount I receive from SSI and SSA in no way is equal to a cost-of-living level.

And I get that my mom **still** pays for stuff for me but that she is also trying to get me set up for when she is no longer here. (She doesn't know that I know that she doesn't use the money I give her for groceries or our shared bills. I know she squirrels it away to save for me in a sock or something for emergency purposes when needed.)

The three of us, my mom, Mary and I just recently we went to a disabled and 'people over 50' fair and gathered tons of information about things we didn't know were available to me. We collected brochures and talked to every representative we could. As a result, I have a second phone-meeting with Cal-Fresh next month to receive food assistance and an EBT card. I've hooked up with a company called Shield HealthCare—medical supplies for home-care—that now provides me with my paper products as well as other medical supplies when needed. I don't know if I have touched on the topic of life-line discounts, but we have always had a reduced electric bill because of having to charge my wheelchair and operate the lift to get me from one place to another and because I am temperature-sensitive. After going to this fair and talking to PG&E, low and behold, we now have a reduced gas bill, something also considered a life-supporting utility. My mom always says that if I could, I would crawl into the fireplace to get warm during the winter.

I have to say, if you or anyone you know happens to be in a similar situation to mine, by all means go to all the fairs; check out all the things; ask all the questions, and don't stop until you get the answers that suit your needs. Who cares if you are the youngest person at the 'people over 50' fair. I now have a file full of pamphlets advertising services, with contact information, that I don't need at the moment but may need in the future. I call it my 'now I need that file' file.

Firsts, ya, firsts, that's where I was . . .money is so disruptive.

***

I think one of my favorite firsts is when Mary and I went to get matching tattoos. After we got to the place my mom felt left-out, or something, and decided that she wanted one, too. Ohana is the tattoo we went after, meaning family, but we chose the word, not because we are blood-family, but because we choose to be friend-family (not anything like Sharon trying to be part of my family, for reals, calling herself kid-four: to this day, Mary and I will catch ourselves saying, "Sharon not OHANA!").

A super big first for me is having someone other than my mom to talk to about . . .all kind of things. Mary is not just my care-provider anymore; she is truly my 'framly.' Nothing is off-limits between us as far as subjects and conversations go. I mean, I know as much about her and her life as she does about me and my life . . .probably to the point of TMI, if truth be known. She has given me someone to bitch-to about my mother, which is such a refreshing and relieving outlet. Seriously, name one person who wants to talk-smack to their mom about their mom, at any age, and who comes away either alive or not feeling like shit. Trust me, having a safe-place to vent (and knowing whatever I say to Mary will not be repeated) is game-changing, even when the smack-talking is about my biggest and best advocate, my mom, the one person who loves me most in the whole-wide-world, who would protect me with her life and who is probably capable of murder on my behalf.

The simple firsts, the everyday firsts, are just as big as the monumental, humongous firsts I've happily and excitedly experienced. The funny thing is, they mostly have to do with time: my entire life, my mother and I have shared our time, together. That statement doesn't make sense, I know, but early on, we devised a time-plan for ourselves so that we both got what we needed or wanted during a day or week or whatever chunk of time we were scheduling.

Our strategy was: I get the morning, and she gets the afternoon; I get today, and she gets tomorrow and so-forth. This was before I had what I now call being on Mary-time, which translates to . . .I have no time limit at all other than being home at 4:30 in the afternoon so that Mary can go home, herself.

As a rule, both Mom and I generally have way more on our to-do lists than either one of us has time for during any-given self-imposed scheduled-slot (of what I have recently dubbed 'Mom-time').

Because of that, my mom, more often than not, in an effort to save time and speed us along, has always kind-of helped me in and out of doorways, in and out of the van, from the van to the store and through any other obstacle that might slow us down, like we are always and forever in a hurry.

It's not that we didn't know before Mary became my arms, legs and transport system (so to speak) that that—the whole helping is not helping thing—was an issue; we did, but Mom and I both have come to realize that she—again, for convivence and the sake of time—helps me too much, has always helped me too much, sometimes . . .which really isn't helping me at all.

Enter Mary, and during our six-and-half-hour day, time is so very irrelevant. She doesn't care if it takes me an hour to get through the front door to the van. Different than my mom needing to accomplish things in a timely fashion (as a mom she just has shit to do), Mary encourages me, every chance she gets, to do what I can for myself when I can, which is mostly driving myself from one place to another, safely, without falling off a sidewalk or running into the side of a building.

(I still comfortably slide into Mom-time when Mary has days off, and Mom-time verses Mary-time has actually gotten closer to being the same thing.)

"Ya, why not? We've got all day, remember?"

So from that first day forward, Mary gives me time and makes or allows me to get in and out of the front door by myself, unless I have to pee, and then I ask for help. (I actually do a lot of stuff based on if I have to pee or not.) We've taken to going for walks for me to get the practice of driving distances (in a straight-line) in the park or down the street to a variety of stores, learning how to properly use crosswalks, for one thing, so I don't get hit. Mary's biggest concern and pet-peeve when we are out and about, walking, shopping, even sitting still, is people being assholes (her words, not mine).

Getting back to new things and experiences, I need to share more about Mary's newly discovered and awareness of people's attitudes and action/reactions to disabled people. She gets absolutely livid when we are out in public and people literally walk over me, like I'm not even there. This is something my mom and I have delt with for years, and Mom just sort of chuckled when Mary and I came home from a shopping trip where a woman almost ended up in my lap, her boobs defiantly and definitely in my face, because I was in her way and she needed to be where I was to pick out the perfect candle. Meanwhile, I was trying to keep my hands down and somewhere near my lap trying not to break any of the glass candle-holders. Mary went off on the lady in total disbelief, saying something like, "Lady, WTF, how do you not see my friend and her six-hundred-pound wheelchair!?"

"Oh, oh, I didn't see her," was the woman's response.

"Stupid is as stupid does!" Mary spat. "I can't believe people! HOW RUDE!!!"

And just as funny to me, but still even more infuriating to Mary, are the people, usually little old ladies, who come up and pat me on top of my head like I'm a tea-cup cockapoo or over-grown three-year-old with no smarts whatsoever and say, "You're such a good girl."

To which Mary inevitably throws out, "She has her Master's Degree and has written thirteen books. What have you done?" and then walks away.

Then there was the time we stopped at CVS to get pictures printed. Let me set the stage:

> The local high school is directly across the street from CVS. The CVS parking lot seems to be, to every parent of every student at that school, the only place to park, wait, hover or drive around and around in circles until said kid makes his or her

appearance. Now, the CVS parking lot is pretty good size, but, dollars-to-donuts, every handicapped parking space is taken by one of these waiting parents with their motors running WITHOUT A SINGLE HANDICAPPED PLACARD OR LICENSE PLATE displayed.

Mary and I became Facebook famous over that one, as a woman sat in her car and watched while we had to park in a non-handicapped space and Mary attempted to drop down the back-load ramp and not get run over. Here is the actual post from a, I want to call her law-abiding, sympathetic, wonderfully aware individual:

> *Yesterday, while waiting for my daughter at the CVS on East Ave, I observed a woman expressing frustration with the driver of a white truck who had*

parked in a designated handicap space without proper authorization. This is a reminder to all PV parents: our children are fully capable of walking a little further if nearby parking spaces are unavailable. Let's be more mindful and considerate of others.

I don't know who this lady is, but I love her.

***

With all the kudos I've given Mary, it doesn't mean we haven't had our tiffs and misunderstandings. We have. That being said, though, I don't actually remember with any clarity any of the specifics of what we fought about or didn't see eye to eye on. I do remember, however, being scared shitless the first time I confronted Mary about . . .something she had done? . . .that I had a problem with. I just knew, like with Sharon (not that I was upset with her quitting on-the-spot), Mary was going to up and quit the second I said something she didn't like.

The day that I decided to talk to Mary about . . .whatever it was, she could tell the moment she walked through the door that something was off. She kept asking me why I was so quiet, and I would blow her off until the spicey chick that Mary single-handedly fostered and brought to life inside of me stepped up and blurted out what my issue with her was. Her response was (and I'm going to say this as bluntly as she said it) "Why the fuck did that take you so long to tell me?"

"Because I was afraid that you would quit just like Sharon did."

"I'm not Sharon. You want coffee?"

Now whenever either of us has a problem, we get it out in the open, first thing, usually over coffee and a brownie.

And that is why after, I don't know how many years, my mom is taking a solo trip, I mean all by herself, without me, my dog or all of my necessary shit, to visit my brother, my sister-in-law and their new-born baby girl. Mary has provided for my mom the bond of 'trust' she needed before she could take the leap of leaving me over-night in someone else's care. Since my dad's passing, my mom and I have had so many firsts, some taken quickly and some very slowly . . . I mean really slowly. This last one, the handing me over totally to someone, not her, while she is three-hours away, has been a long time coming. This is the most gigantic-ist ever FIRST, specifically for my mom. I'm secretly holding my breath that she doesn't chicken out. I have faith, though, that she has enough guts, grit and trust for the both of us in this whole new step forward in life to go meet Baby Bean and feel comfortable leaving me behind, alone but not alone.

Now Mary and I just need to keep our mouths shut about what we have planned for those forty-eight hours Mom will be gone. It isn't like she doesn't know that we have plans. She just doesn't really want to know.

Mom did say the other day, "I can't think about it, leaving you to your own devices, because it stresses me out. It makes me worry that I will be that far away and can't get to you if I need to . . .not like I could when I'm gone . . .

. . ., like gone-gone."

Epilogue

My mom's trip happened. She didn't chicken-out. We spent an entire, continuous thirty-hours apart from each other. I am in one piece, and my mother's pot of stress is much smaller. All of the things she fretted about were not the insurmountable obstacles she thought they would be: the leaving me in the care of someone else for more than six or seven hours at a time, the drive, by herself, on Highway 20 (super, curvy road around Clear Lake), being three hours away from home if there was an emergency—all legitimate concerns, but I have to say, really unfounded. Mary always has my back, so I on the other hand, had no concerns about my care, whatsoever.

Although, we, I, did have Mom-Vision (Life360) open while she was driving so that Mary and I knew when she had arrived at both destinations: my brother's house and back home in Chico. As soon as I got the first texted picture of Mom and Aida Bean, I knew that my mom's eyes were leaking happy tears and probably not so worried about me, again trusting in "My Mary" with me.

The next big thing—me leaving Mom for a late-evening event, two-hours away from home with Mary and a new friend, Byron, as our designated driver and protector, if needed. I'm pretty sure this will stir Mom's pot a little, but I'm also sure she will survive.

A photo album of Firsts

Being on Mom-time . . .

her driving me in the rain.

First walk to CVS

First time EVER skating

Yup! Matching tattoos!

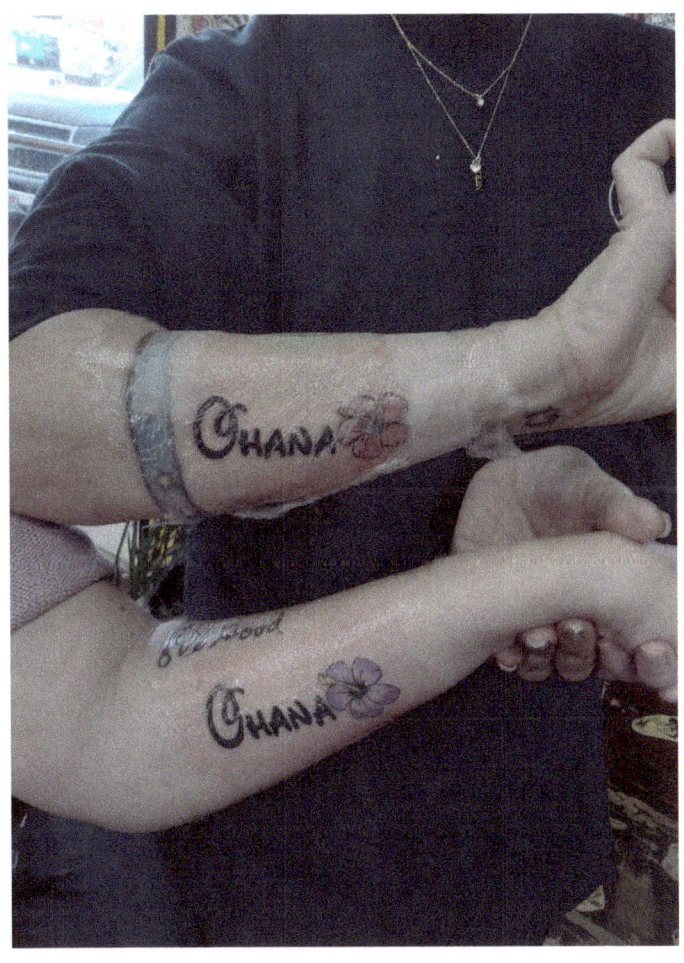

Dressed to the nines!

This is why we were dressed to the nines!

Me and the HUNKS!

Checking out the fancy "powder room."

Need I explain.

Working Out—

A girls gotta do what a girls gotta do.

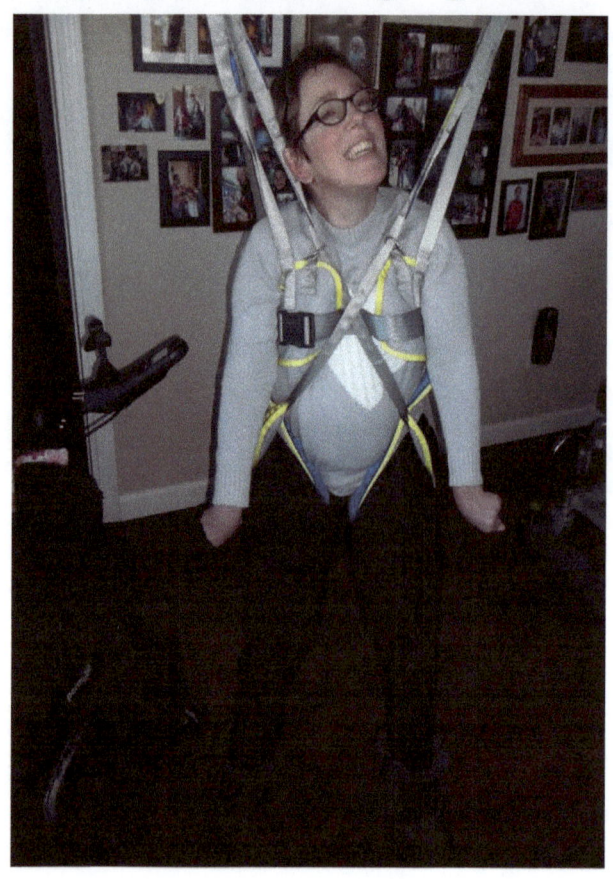

Even working out is fun!

Let me show you what it is like being me.

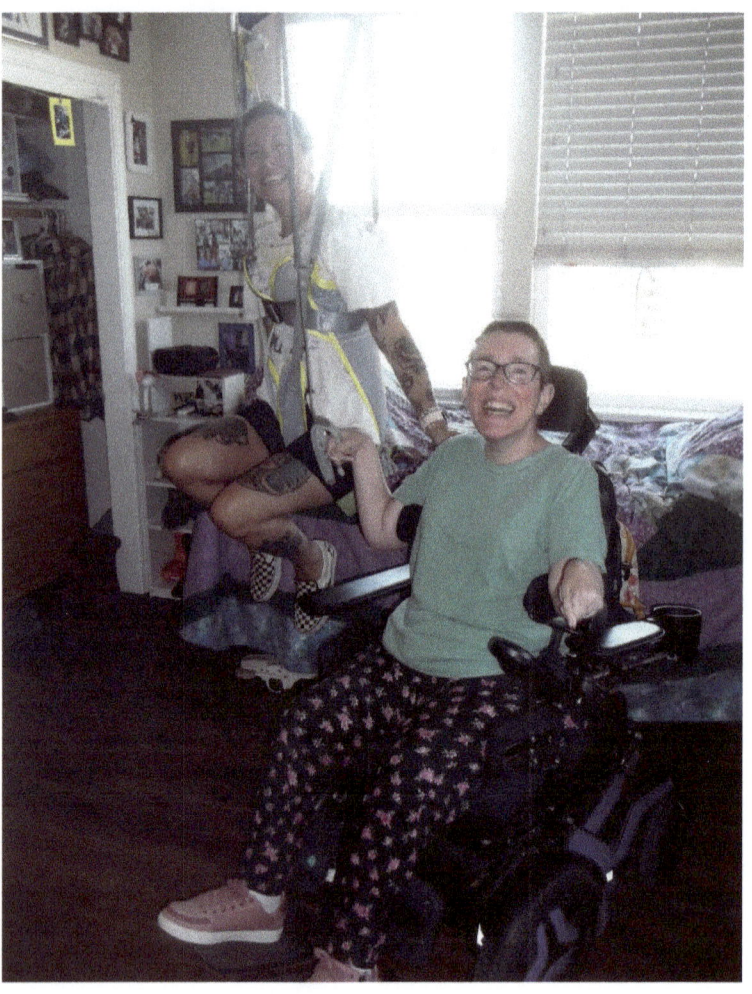

Having Mary experience a disability.

She didn't like it!

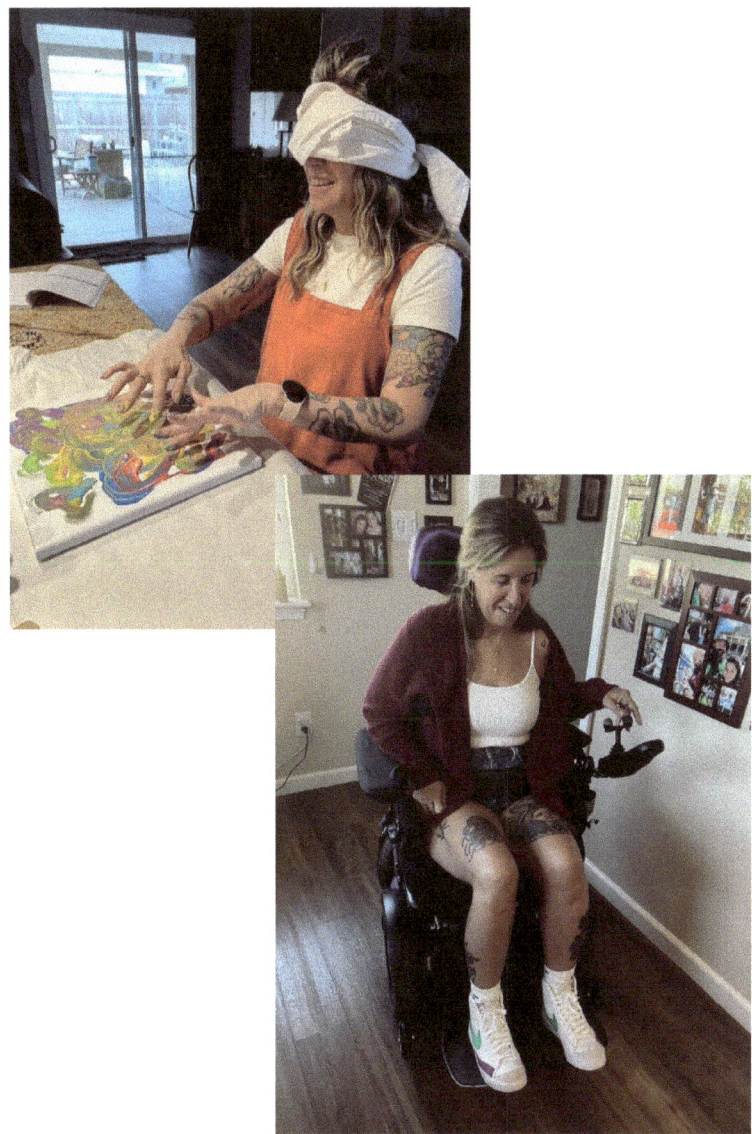

Me teaching Mary how to do Abstract Expressionism painting.

Checking out the new Taylor Swift, *Tortured Poet Society* Album.

. . .one of us is a Swifty

Fun at lunch . . .

Making Christmas cookies . . .

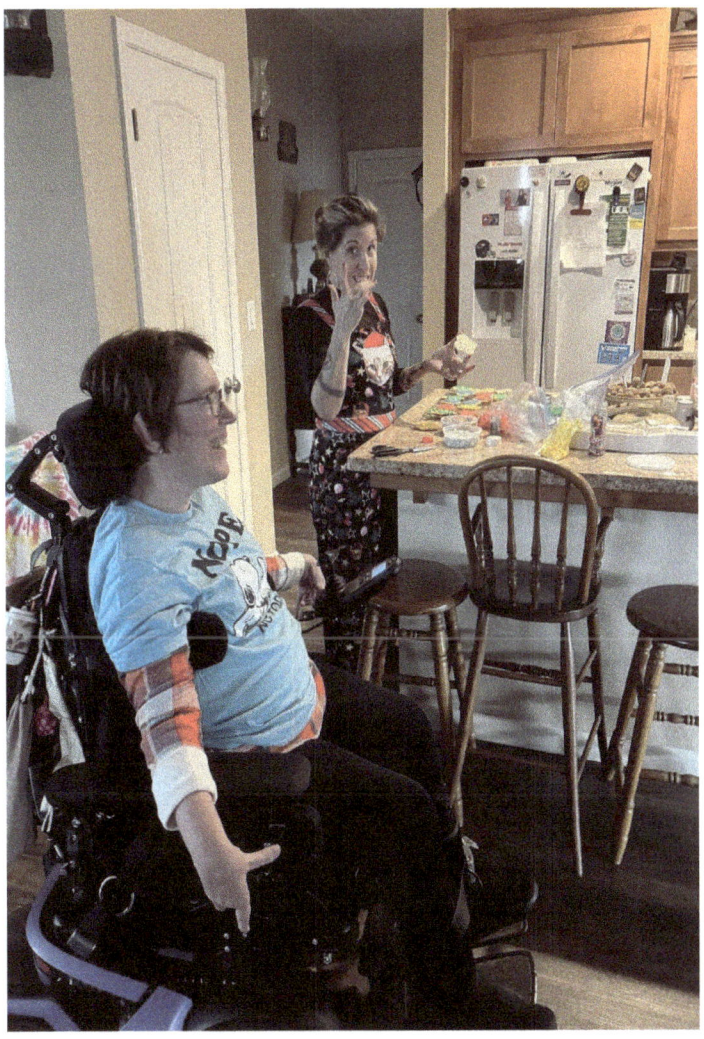

Ax throwing...1, 2, 3 throw!

How we kick it. . .

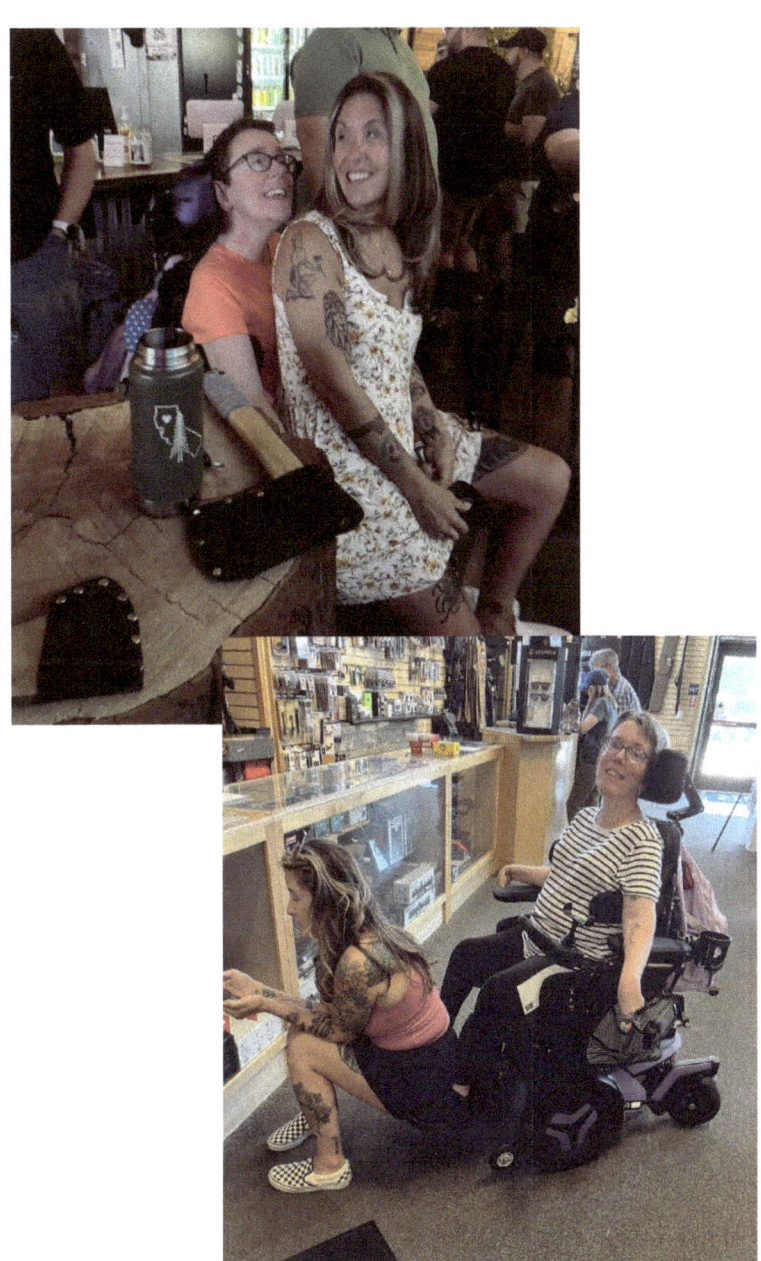

A Halloween unicorn and her witch (and her black magic dog).

Christmas jammies movie day

Sharing my latest children's book.

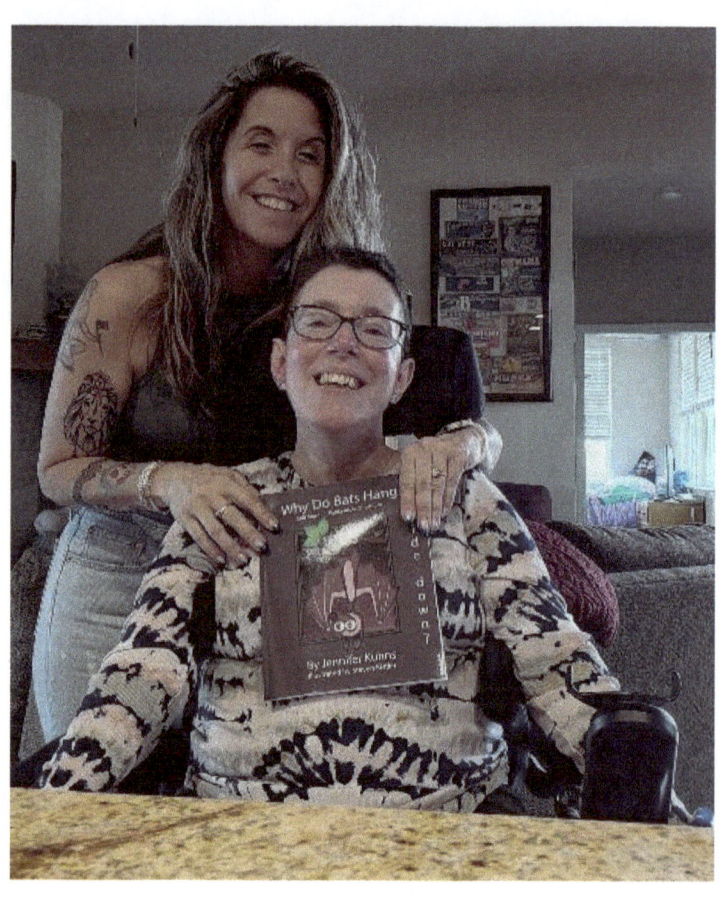

Selling books in Author's Alley.

My first toe job!

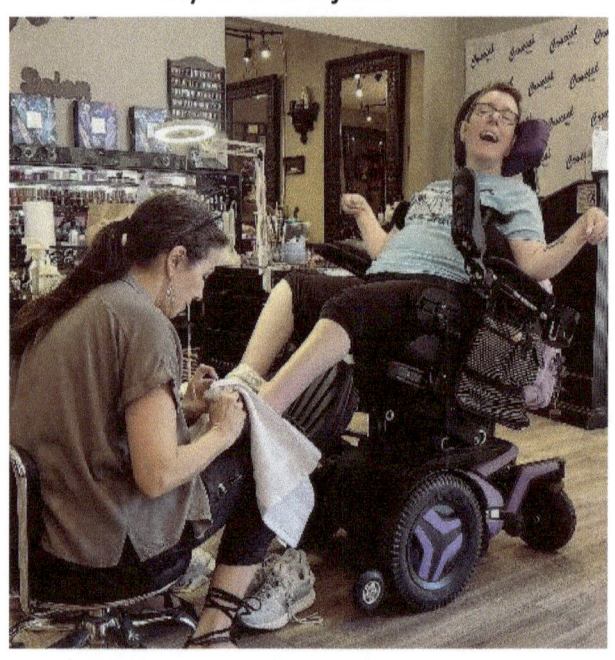

My second toe job.

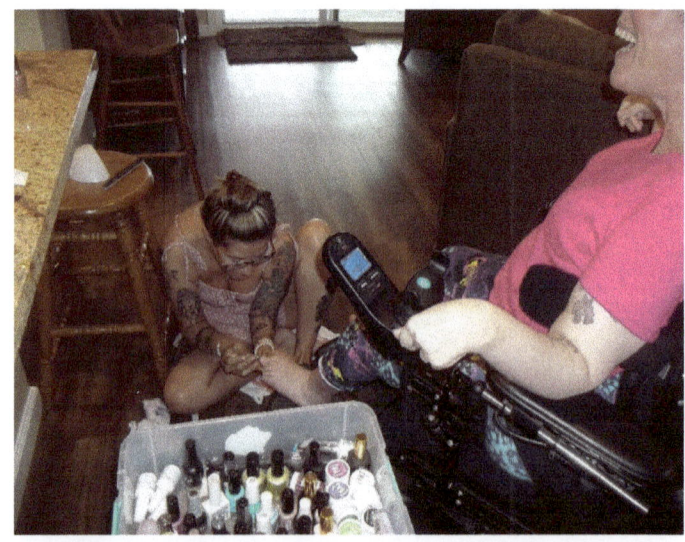

Getting a little help signing books.

The three of us . . .me and the two who are probably capable of murder on my behalf.

The Divas with Daiquiris!

More books by Jennifer Kuhns

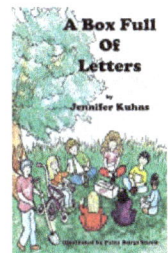

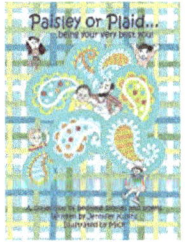
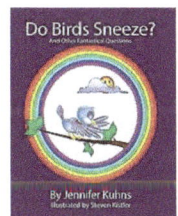

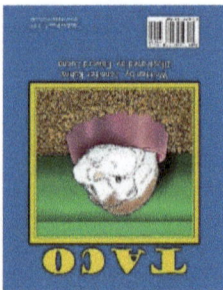

A two-sided flipbook

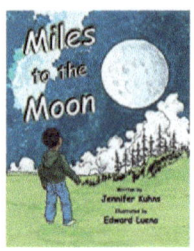
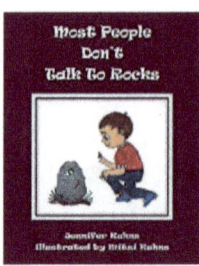

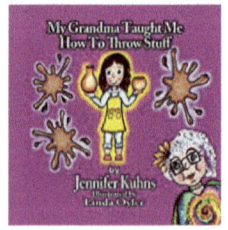

For the adult reader . . .parts one
and two of her autobiography

www.ingramcontent.com/pod-product-compliance
Lightning Source LLC
Chambersburg PA
CBHW051515120626
46551CB00012B/940